The Columbus of the Woods

The Columbus of the Woods

Daniel Boone and the Typology
of Manifest Destiny

J. Gray Sweeney

*An Exhibition Commemorating
the Columbian Quincentenary*

The Washington University Gallery of Art
St. Louis, Missouri

The Washington University Gallery of Art
Steinberg Hall
St. Louis, Missouri 63130

This exhibition and publication have been made
possible by the generous grant of funds from the following
institutions and individuals:

Hortense Lewin Art Fund of Washington University

Arizona State University

Sylvia and Abraham Krissoff

Missouri Arts Council

Cover: George C. Bingham, *Daniel Boone Escorting Settlers*
Through the Cumberland Gap.
1851-52. Oil on Canvas, 36 1/2" x 50 1/4". Washington University
Gallery of Art, St. Louis. Gift of Nathaniel Phillips, 1890.

Catalogue Design: Suzanne Oberholtzer
Catalogue Editing: Gretchen Lee
Catalogue Production: Roberta Stege

ISBN 0-936316-14-4

There hung for many months, on the walls of the Art-Union gallery in New York, a picture ... so thoroughly national in its subject and true to nature in execution, that it was refreshing to contemplate it .... It represented a flat ledge of rock, the summit of a high cliff that projected over a rich, umbrageous country, upon which a band of hunters leaning on their rifles, were gazing with looks of delighted surprise. The foremost ... is pointing out the landscape to his comrades, with an air of exultant yet calm satisfaction ... his loose hunting shirt, his easy attitude, the fresh brown tint of his cheek, and an ingenuous, cheerful, determined yet benign expression of countenance, proclaim the hunter and pioneer, the Columbus of the woods, the forest philosopher and brave champion. The picture represents Daniel Boone discovering to his companions the fertile levels of Kentucky.

Henry T. Tuckerman,
The Western Pioneer, 1852

To the Memory of David C. Huntington, 1922-1990
Excited Spirit of American Art

Contents

Lenders to the Exhibition

A.G. Edwards and Sons, Inc., St. Louis

The People of Missouri through The Bingham Trust, St. Louis

The Thomas Gilcrease Institute of American History and Art,
Tulsa, Oklahoma

The Massachusetts Historical Society, Boston

The Mead Art Museum, Amherst College,
Amherst, Massachusetts

The St. Louis Mercantile Library Association, St. Louis

The Missouri Historical Society, St. Louis

The Museum of Fine Arts, Springfield, Massachusetts

The National Museum of American Art,
Smithsonian Institution, Washington, D.C.

The New-York Historical Society, New York

Mr. Arthur J. Phelan

The St. Louis Art Museum, St. Louis

Special Collections, Olin Library,
Washington University, St. Louis

Private Collection

Foreword

In recognition of the quincentenary of Columbus's encounter with the "New World," the Washington University Gallery of Art organized the exhibition *The Columbus of the Woods: Daniel Boone and the Typology of Manifest Destiny* and published this catalogue. In his role as explorer and discoverer of new lands, Daniel Boone came to be equated with Christopher Columbus and was described by the art critic Henry T. Tuckerman in 1852 as "the Columbus of the woods." The landing of Christopher Columbus on the island of San Salvador in 1492 was a decisive event in European history, initiating the expansion of Europe's imperial powers and their colonization in this hemisphere. For the native peoples of the Americas the spectacular appearance of the white sails rising in the Eastern seas marked the dawn of their eventual demise at the hand of the European conquerors. Mid-19th-century descendants of the colonizers in the United States viewed Boone's march into Kentucky as a pivotal event in their expansion westward to dominate the continent—an expansion that they equated with Columbus's. Certainly, for Native Americans the appearance of Boone with his flintlock rifle signaled an end to Native American society in North America, as had the appearance of Columbus for Central and South American natives.

In the United States, especially after the War of 1812, the frontier was pushed farther west by the spiritual and entrepreneurial descendants of Columbus—fur-trappers, mountain men, and pioneers hungry for rich lands. As the new nation sought to construct narratives to represent its emerging national identity, the daring frontiersmen who led the advancing Anglo-European civilization gained recognition as heroes in literature and the visual arts. A central persona in the nation's search for its identity was Daniel Boone. Even in his own time the tale of Boone's role as the leader of colonists migrating through the Cumberland Gap into the Kentucky territories had begun to assume larger-than-life status. Due to the zeal of several generations of writers and artists, Boone came to be considered the consummate symbol of the American pioneer in the decades prior to the Civil War. By the 1850s tales of this real estate speculator, hunter, and Indian killer had expanded into mythic proportions and he became famous as "the pathfinder." As this study demonstrates, by the 1850s Boone had become a symbol of America's self-proclaimed Manifest Destiny. It was in this context that visual images of Daniel Boone achieved greatest circulation and were widely celebrated in popular illustrations and paintings.

Daniel Boone's importance in American art and literature has long been acknowledged by scholars such as Henry Nash Smith and Richard Slotkin. Slotkin particularly argued that Boone was "the most significant, most emotionally compelling myth-hero of the early Republic." When Professor J. Gray Sweeney approached me with a proposal to mount an exhibition on the theme of Daniel Boone, I was surprised to learn that a study interpreting the Boone myth in 19th-century American art had never been undertaken. This exhibition assembles virtually all of the major images of Daniel Boone in American art of this period, and in his essay Professor Sweeney has constructed a compelling analysis of the iconography of Boone—from the first and only life portrait by Chester Harding through the metamorphosis of Boone in the paintings of Thomas Cole, William T. Ranney, George Caleb Bingham, Carl Wimar, and Emanuel Leutze. His study uncovers numerous connections between the depiction of Boone in popular literature and his representation in history paintings, and it shows how the artists' images of the pioneer were linked to the social and political issues of the period. Professor Sweeney's discussion of Boone illuminates the importance of Boone imagery for 19th-century American culture, as a symbol of the American belief in their destiny to expand across the continent and colonize Native American territories, just as Columbus had.

The quincentenary of Columbus's encounter with the "New World" provides an opportunity for a comprehensive review of "the Columbus of the woods" in American art of the pre-Civil War period. Furthermore, 1992-93 marks the centennial of Frederick Jackson Turner's pronouncement of his "Frontier Thesis" that launched the modern age of scholarship about the American West.

The coincidence of these events provides an additional stimulus to reconsider the traditionally accepted accounts of Daniel Boone, highlighting his important role in the history of American art. Since the 1880s Washington University has held George Caleb Bingham's painting of *Daniel Boone Escorting Settlers Through the Cumberland Gap* (1851-52). It is the centerpiece of the exhibition and one of the most complex and influential expressions of 19th-century America's fascination with Boone. The Gallery of Art also holds Carl Wimar's renowned painting of *The Abduction of Daniel Boone's Daughter by the Indians* (1853), a work closely entwined with the myth of Boone in the decade before the Civil War. In addition, the extensive resources of the Special Collections at Washington University's Olin Library, with the rich collections of the St. Louis Mercantile Library Association and the Missouri Historical Society, have been drawn upon to provide copies of important texts, documents, and popular illustrations to complete this study of Boone. It must also be remembered that Boone chose Missouri as his final home, spending the last two decades of his life in the state where he died in 1820, which allows Missouri more than a passing claim on the legacy of Boone. In light of these factors, it is entirely appropriate that the Washington University Gallery of Art should organize this exhibition.

This landmark exhibition could not have been realized without the efforts of many people across the United States, whose contributions I wish to acknowledge. Various institutional and private lenders generously lent their paintings, drawings, prints, and books for this project. Marny Sandweiss, director of the Mead Art Museum, Amherst College; Louis Tucker, director of the Massachusetts Historical Society; the late Fred Myers, director of the Thomas Gilcrease Museum of American History and Art; Hollister Sturges, director of the Springfield Museum of Fine Arts; and Betsy Brown, director, and William Truettner, curator, of the National Museum of American Art were very accommodating in assisting with the loans of their important paintings of Daniel Boone. Private lenders also made the sacrifice of permitting their cherished works of art to be shared with the public for this project.

The primary support for this project was provided by the Hortense Lewin Art Fund of Washington University. Established in 1984 by Tobias Lewin in memory of his wife, this fund has enabled the Gallery of Art to produce a major exhibition and catalog each year since its inception. I am also grateful to Mrs. Sylvia Kryssoff and to Arizona State University for generously supporting the publication. Additional funds were provided by the Institute of Museum Services, a federal agency; the Missouri Arts Council, a state agency; and the Regional Arts Commission, a local agency. I would like to commend the staff at the Gallery of Art for diligent attention to the production of the exhibition, catalog, and programs. I especially wish to thank Gray Sweeney who has given wholeheartedly to this project.

Joseph D. Ketner
Director
Washington University Gallery of Art

Acknowledgments

Many individuals have assisted me during the time I was preparing this exhibition, and it is a pleasure to acknowledge them. Without the strong support of Joseph D. Ketner, Director of the Gallery of Art, the exhibition could never have occurred. His wholehearted support of this study is commended with my best thanks. His appreciation of the potential for an in-depth study of Daniel Boone in the visual arts has made it possible for this investigation to reach fruition.

Special thanks are extended to Sylvia and Abraham Krissoff of Grand Rapids, Michigan, for their generous support of the exhibition catalogue. At Arizona State University I would like to thank The Office of Research and Creative Activity for support of the preliminary research for the project, and my colleagues Julie Codell, Director, and Jon Share, Assistant Director of the School of Arts, and Seymour Rosen, Dean of the College of Fine Arts, for providing additional funds for the publication. Professors Corine Schleif and Nancy Serwint were helpful in providing thoughtful responses to my queries for information. I would particularly like to acknowledge the dedicated help of my Research Assistant Pamela Belanger who has been of unfailing assistance with the bibliography and endnotes. Without the enthusiastic support of Arizona State University the exhibition could have never been realized.

In St. Louis I would like to thank Holly Hall, Director of Special Collections at the Olin Library, for her generous assistance with materials on Daniel Boone from the Bryan Collection, and John Hoover at the St. Louis Mercantile Library Association for his help with additional rare materials from that collection. Duane Snedecker at the Missouri Historical Society has been generous in supplying materials from the Society's collections.

I would like to acknowledge the contributions of several scholars who have assisted me in completing the catalogue essay. Leah Lipton at Framingham State College has generously shared her knowledge of Chester Harding with me. Robert Mugerauer at the University of Texas, Austin,

has shared additional insights about contemporary hermeneutics. Merl M. Moore generously provided important archival material. Alan Wallach of The College of William and Mary has thoughtfully commented on the manuscript, as has James C. Moore at the Albuquerque Museum. Michael DeMarsche of Chatham College responded to an early draft of the essay, and Arthur J. Phelan offered helpful comments on the text. John Mack Faragher of Mount Holyoke College clarified key points about Boone's biography. Jane E. Neidhardt, administrative assistant at the Gallery of Art, capably assisted with editing and proofreading. My thanks to all these individuals for their assistance.

Additional scholars whose publications have been influential in preparing this study of Daniel Boone's image in the visual arts are: Sacvan Bercovitch of Harvard University, the late E. Maurice Bloch at the University of California at Los Angeles, William H. Goetzmann of the University of Texas, Dawn Glanz at Bowling Green State University, Vivien Fryd Green of Vanderbilt University, Francis S. Grubar at George Washington University, Patricia Hills at Boston University, the late David C. Huntington at the University of Michigan, Elizabeth Johns of the University of Pennsylvania, Michael A. Lofaro at the University of Kentucky, Nancy Rash at Connecticut College, Richard Slotkin at Wesleyan University, and William H. Truettner at the National Museum of American Art.

Above all, I cannot sufficiently express my thanks to my wife Karrie and my son James for their enduring patience and understanding during the long period when this study was in progress. Without their support this publication could never have become a reality.

J. Gray Sweeney
Professor of Art History
School of Art and Art History
Arizona State University

Artist unknown, *Daniel Boone Hunting in the Wilds of Kentucke*,
Special Collections, Olin Library, Washington University, St. Louis.

Daniel Boone and American Art

For many Americans today the name Daniel Boone conjures up a vivid picture of the "pathfinder." Striding forth at the head of a column of settlers, Boone has become a figure larger than life as he moves through a stormy mountain pass to fulfill the promise of a new life on the Western frontier. This stereotyped recollection of Boone has become a permanent fixture of the American historical imagination, and innumerable references to Boone in scholarly articles, books on American history, and school texts are ample evidence of a traditional acceptance of him as a genuine national hero.[1] Despite Boone's legendary reputation, confusion still exists about his relationship to his historical period, and there is uncertainty about how and why he achieved his persisting popular reputation.

The exhibition confirms that Boone's enduring fame as part of 20th-century American consciousness is largely a legacy of 19th-century writers and artists. Rather than celebrate the conventional reverence for Daniel Boone as a folk hero of mythic proportions, this inquiry explores how and why talents of painters, print makers and sculptors were enlisted to nourish one of the great empire building inventions of pre-Civil War America —the image of Daniel Boone, the "Columbus of the woods," as a critic of the 1850s described him.

The centerpiece of this exhibition is George Caleb Bingham's *Daniel Boone Escorting Settlers Through the Cumberland Gap*, painted 1851–52 **(Cover, Figure 28)**. It is the most frequently reproduced and widely admired painting of the legendary pioneer in American art, and a work that contributed decisively to the process of creating the Boone legend. Bingham's image was created at the height of America's expansion into the West under the banner of Manifest Destiny. Encoded in this picture were complicated social and political ideas about Boone as the exemplar of westward expansion. Recovering these now-obscured meanings provides a stimulus for a new interpretation of other depictions of Daniel Boone.

This is the first exhibition to scrutinize the reputation of Daniel Boone in 19th-century American art. Although

there have been numerous exhibitions and monographs about the West in American art, the figure of Boone—the quintessential pioneer—has largely eluded methodical analysis by art historians. This study attempts to rectify that omission by collecting all the significant images of Daniel Boone extant, and subjecting them to revisionist analysis. Specific sources in contemporary texts are uncovered that help to explain how the artists' images acquired their meanings, what audiences were attracted by these pictures, and what power they possessed to rationalize and motivate behavior. The most puzzling aspect of Boone's reputation in the visual arts is that fewer than a dozen major works depict him, despite his enormous popularity in literature.[2]

Artists adapted and manipulated the figure of Daniel Boone as a vanguard type of Western pioneer to serve a variety of agendas. These ranged from an atypical Federalist depiction by Thomas Cole of Boone as a hermit rejecting the advance of civilization, to the theatrical gestures of William Ranney's representation of Boone claiming dominion over new lands through the power of vision, to George Caleb Bingham's Boone, a Moses-like figure heading a column of Anglo-Saxon families migrating west to settle. Appeals for national consensus, visually expressed in the elaborate painted rhetoric of Emanuel Leutze's *Westward the Course of Empire Takes Its Way* **(Color Plate 4, Figure 44)**, found Boone diminished from preeminent protagonist to a venerable prophet whose heroic deeds more than half a century earlier had foreshadowed a new transcontinental empire. Tracing how the symbol of Boone was reconstructed by artists before the Civil War discloses the shifting meaning of the pioneer as a symbol of the search for national understanding about the meaning of the Western frontier, and helps to explain why after about 1861 Daniel Boone virtually disappears from the visual arts.

Unlike orthodox accounts of the "pathfinder" popular during the 1950s and 1960s, this inquiry will not accept a literal reading of these visual artifacts as illustrations of heroic feats that are traditionally claimed to have been the foundation of American greatness. Nor will it fall into "reification," the fallacy of treating these images and the myths they represent as straightforward representations of the reality they purport to describe. The methodology used here is one of contemporary hermeneutics: the recognition that behind all artistic expressions lurk interpretations of the real, and that reality is always partially seen within cultural horizons and transformed in art and literature in order to serve the interests of power. Hans-Georg Gadamer, the leading theoretician of hermeneutics, observes, "Nothing that is [painted] has its truth simply in itself, but refers instead backward and forward to what is unsaid."[3] As Friedrich Nietzsche more bluntly put it a century ago, "Facts is [sic] precisely what there is not, only interpretations."[4]

Among the issues that emerge through study of the visual artifacts representing the Boone myth are: the belief that "great men" like Boone acted as "instruments of Providence;" the conflict between the pioneer as an agent of progress subduing the Indian but simultaneously tempted by primitivism; and faith in a typological model as an explanation of national history, in which biblical precedent, it was believed, could confer divine authority on American expansion to the West.

Problems of race and gender also appear, for Daniel Boone was a white male hero, who would inspire James

Artist unknown, *Daniel Boone*, engraved by Doolittle & Munson, Special Collections, Olin Library, Washington University, St. Louis.

Fenimore Cooper's Natty Bumppo and help to infuse additional meaning into the tall tales of Davy Crockett. As a renowned hunter, scout and "Indian killer," Boone symbolized nearly every aspect of frontier mythology for several generations, although at times artists and writers expressed fears that he might have become more Indian-like than his Native American adversaries. Boone would assume many contradictory identities: by turns he might be a stealthy Indian-like hunter, a scout or explorer, a fierce Indian-killer, a land speculator, a politician, and in perhaps his most improbable role, a settler establishing a permanent abode for his family on the frontier. In all of his various guises, Boone was ennobled to the stature of a hero who articulated aspects of the American desire to establish a lasting home on the frontier.

His first biographer, John Filson, presented him as early as 1784 as a providentially invested figure carrying out a divine mandate to bring civilization to a hostile wilderness. With varying degrees of emphasis, Boone's role as a leader of this army of expansion become his central persona—the indelible emblem of the "pathfinder." Artists and writers celebrated Boone as a great frontier hero. Their strategies went far beyond simply acclaiming his tenacity and cunning in wresting land from the Native Americans and carving out homesteads for hungry pioneers.

Boone's many hagiographers transformed him from an unsophisticated, almost illiterate, frontiersman and inept real estate speculator into a symbol of the workings of Providence unfolding America's national destiny. Most 19th-century Americans subscribed unashamedly to notions of progress. The authority of an unlimited conviction in human perfectibility and national progress lay behind much of the symbolism of Boone in his many personas. Americans of the early-19th century craved heroes who would signify their faith in this boundless future to transact what Sacvan Bercovitch has termed a "ritual of consensus." They yearned for symbols, both visual and written, to connect the unpredictable future and turbulent present with the certainties of the past, especially those described in their most venerated book, the Bible.

In order to conceptualize these longed-for connections between the biblical past and the nation's future, promoters of westward expansion often relied on the series of ideas expressed in the symbolic language of typology. Typology originated in the Medieval study of scriptural types, but Americans expanded the idea to embrace the notion that contemporary happenings could be interpreted as if they had been foreshadowed by biblical events and personages. Typology allowed the zealous effort to fill the continent with an entrepreneurial civilization to be invested with a spiritual and historical precedent. With typology the desire to discern connections between the great issues and events of the day by drawing parallels with prophetic types from the Bible became a powerful device for motivating and justifying the course of an expanding American empire.

In the turbulent decades before the Civil War, many Americans were eager to subscribe to the idea of typology. They welcomed the anthropocentric notion that their country was the focus of a prophesied order of history in which the sacred and the secular were indivisible. Americans before the Civil War were excited by the belief that history, nature, and contemporary events were all visible revelations of a divine plan.[5] Moreover, for a nation increasingly divided by powerful sectional and class tensions, anxious about the expansion of slavery to Western territories, and uncertain about the emergence of industrialization and urbanization, typology fulfilled a deep longing for consensus about the American mission.[6] The result was acceptance of typological thinking among many classes, religious sects, and regions. In the visual arts, as in literature and politics, typology became a fashionable vehicle for justifying and cloaking what was often merely a self-serving program of unfettered imperial expansion.

The Jacksonian Democrats of the early-19th century shifted the meaning of the frontier from a secular or geographical barrier, the border dividing one people from another, to a mythical threshold. The term "frontier" was redefined, as Sacvan Bercovitch observes, through a rhetorical inversion, "to mean a *figural* outpost, the outskirts of the advancing kingdom of God. It became, in short, not a dividing line but a summons to territorial expansion."[7] In Europe the concept of frontier signified boundary and restriction; in America it came to symbolize faith in an unlimited expansion to the West and the consummation of the divine promise to the nation. The frontiersman like Boone—the "pathfinder"—was invested with the sacred mission of moving this outpost of progress further west.

By the 1850s the frontier had changed from a dark, unknown place to one with much allure as terror was overcome by millennial visions of empire and profit. By the end of the century, in his famous 1893 address, *The Significance of the Frontier in American History*, historian Frederick Jackson Turner converted the exhortative power of typology into official orthodoxy as an historical explanation of the frontier as the central symbol of American history. "Stand at the Cumberland Gap," wrote Turner, "and watch the procession of civilization marching single file—the buffalo… the Indian, the fur trader and hunter, the cattle raiser, the pioneer farmer,—and the frontier has passed by."[8] Turner's verbal image has an uncanny resonance with Bingham's painting of Daniel Boone escorting settlers through a dark defile into the West.

An artist working in the 1850s and a historian writing in the 1890s were both inspired by the notion of a divine unfolding of national destiny in which heroic types like Daniel Boone played a key role in defining the ethos of the frontier. The linkage of the mythic figure of Boone and idea of typology provided a potent foundation on which to construct seemingly plausible representations of American history. Interpreting the contributions of the visual arts to this transformative process provides a new perspective on values long considered central to the cultural basis of American identity.

CHAPTER I

Behind the Legend of Daniel Boone

Who or what Daniel Boone really was is less important than the way later generations constructed him to satisfy their cultural and ideological needs. His life as an actual person who lived from 1734 to 1820 almost disappeared under an avalanche of words and images, as the few solidly established facts about him were elaborated to express the changing ideals of a frontier hero. A brief examination of the career of the man Boone, demythologizing his legend, is essential to understanding how and why he became a notable, if occasionally problematic, symbol in the visual arts. In doing this it is possible to observe the process by which a man goes from legend to myth to symbol.

In a recent study, Michael A. Lofaro has distilled basic facts from fiction in an account of Boone's life that avoids the rhetorical fervor so marked in most 19th century versions of his career.[9] Similarly, Richard Slotkin's *Regeneration Through Violence,* has traced in detail the varied representations of Boone in literature, beginning with the first description published by John Filson through the enormously popular 19th century versions of Timothy Flint, John Mason Peck, and others. These literary texts were of crucial importance because they directly influenced the creation of the paintings, prints and sculptures that are the subject of this exhibition.

It would be difficult to discuss the figure of Daniel Boone without acknowledging that his life was, in fact, filled with remarkable adventures. Many of his exploits seem, at least at first glance, to be the stuff of heroism. Whatever else Daniel Boone may have been, he was extraordinary because above all he was a survivor. Boone's years of severe hardship spent in the wilderness were filled with numerous deadly encounters with Native American tribesmen including a prolonged captivity, and the violent death of his sons, brothers, and friends. His numerous brushes with the law and the difficult life of a transient who never settled long in one place were all part of the documented existence of the man. He was famous as a hunter, scout, and explorer, skills much prized in late-18th- and early-19th-century frontier life, and he was one of the finest marksmen of his day. Boone was also a disheartened man because of great fortunes that always

eluded him. His financial troubles stemmed from his naivete about legal formalities or a stubborn unwillingness to submit to them, and from his desire, entirely typical of his period, to become wealthy and successful from impulsive speculation in land development. For all he did to open the West to settlement, Daniel Boone died in poverty, a ward of his surviving sons.

Thanks to several generations of historians the life of Daniel Boone is now well-documented. How to interpret it is another matter. He was born of a family of dissenters, Quakers, from the "middling class" of weavers who emigrated to America in 1717. His father, Squire Boone, was a moderately successful farmer and miller. Daniel was his sixth child, born in Bucks County, Pennsylvania on November 2, 1734. His family apparently named him for the Dutch painter, Daniel Boone, who died in London in 1698, and may have been a distant relative. The famous comment attributed to his father, "Let the girls do the spelling and Dan'l will do the shooting" captured Boone's interest in formal education.[10] The Boone family moved to the extreme western frontier settlement in the Yadkin Valley of North Carolina by 1750. There Daniel Boone began in earnest his life as a frontiersman.

Although Boone became an American hero, it is ironic that he completed much of his career as a frontiersman opening the West during the period of British Colonial rule, and he later lived in Missouri under Spanish authority. During the French and Indian Wars Boone became a wagoner in the Colonial Militia accompanying British General Edward Braddock's march into the Ohio River Valley in 1755. Boone and a friend, John Findley, who had recently returned from scouting in Kentucky, were commanded by Major George Washington. During Braddock's disastrous rout, Boone, at the rear with the supply wagons, saw the regular soldiers fleeing, and decided to cut the traces of his horses and escape. He returned to North Carolina dreaming of easy wealth from taking furs in the territory of Kentucky that Findley had told him about.

At the frontier settlement of Yadkin, Boone and seventeen-year-old Rebecca Bryan married on August 14, 1756. The Boone and Bryan families were to be closely

Color plate 1. Chester Harding, *Daniel Boone*, 1820.
Oil on canvas, 29" x 24". Private collection.

Color plate 2. Thomas Cole, *Daniel Boone at His Cabin at Great Osage Lake*, 1826. Oil on canvas, 38" x 42 1/2". Mead Art Museum, Amherst College, Massachusetts.

Color plate 3. William T. Ranney, *Daniel Boone's First View of Kentucky*, 1849.
Oil on canvas, 36" x 53 1/2". The Thomas Gilcrease Institute of American
History and Art, Tulsa, Oklahoma.

Color plate 4. Emanuel Luetze, *Westward the Course of Empire Takes Its Way*, 1861. Oil on canvas, 33 1/4" x 43 3/8". National Museum of American Art, Washington, D.C. Bequest of Sara Carr Upton.

intertwined, both through marriage and political and economic bonds. In the winter of 1768-1769 John Findley visited Boone again, in North Carolina. He brought with him more stories of easy hunting for furs in Kentucky. Boone had several motives for entering Kentucky, for Lofaro observes, "Daniel's 'scratch' farming, never vigorously pursued, could barely provide for his family."[11] In addition Boone was being sued for unpaid debts owed to Judge Richard Henderson. Henderson emerges as a major figure operating behind the scenes in Boone's Western exploits. Eager to promote land development in Kentucky, Henderson and his Transylvania Land Company needed men to explore the region and try to negotiate its purchase from the Cherokees who possessed the territory by royal treaty. Henderson may have financed Boone's first expedition to Kentucky in 1769 with Findley and three other men.

Untangling facts from legend is difficult when it comes to Boone's several expeditions into Kentucky Territory, "the Dark and Bloody Ground" as the Native Americans called it. The key source of information about the period from 1769 to 1782 is found in Boone's putative "autobiography." Ghost-written by John Filson, who had earlier interviewed Boone for the chapter "The Adventures of Col. Daniel Boone," the account appeared in Filson's book *The Discovery, Settlement And Present State of Kentucke*, first published in 1784 **(Figure 1)**.[12] Filson's account represented Boone as a forest philosopher in the manner of Rousseau more than the self-interested land speculator, hunter, and Indian fighter who emerges in the biographies of modern historians. Boone's real objective on that first foray into Kentucky was to take as many deerskins as possible to repay the money borrowed from Henderson, and to reconnoiter routes into Indian territories for Henderson's company.

The nasty problem for Boone and his associates on this first expedition was that the animals they hunted and the land they coveted were legally the exclusive property of the Native Americans because of the British Proclamation of 1763, which forbade settlement west of the Alleghenies. The Native Americans were furious when they found Boone and his party taking their game. During this first incursion into Kentucky, Boone ascended the "commanding ridge" that Filson so vividly characterized, to overlook the wealth of Kentucky that he planned to wrest from the Indians. This moment became the basis for William Ranney's two paintings of 1849 **(Color Plate 3, Figures 21, 24)**. Through the winter of 1770 the party hunted with great success, and in the spring Squire Boone, Daniel's brother, returned to North Carolina with the hides they had taken to repay their debts. Daniel remained alone in the wilderness, although a few months later Squire came back with fresh horses and ammunition. Squire's return through hostile Indian territory was depicted by Ranney in his picture of 1852 **(Figure 27)**.

Boone's next attempt to enter and to lay claim to Kentucky occurred in 1773. The attempt ended in disaster. In late September Boone departed for Kentucky with a small party of five families. They planned to follow an established Indian or buffalo trace that was too narrow for a wagon. Moving single-file in a pack-train, many of the party were on foot. One group was headed by Boone's seventeen-year-old son Henry. On the night of October 2, a band of Native Americans attacked them as they slept. Nearly all of the party were killed, and Boone's son Henry was tortured to death. The remainder of the group was so frightened by the grisly scene they encountered the next day that they abandoned their illegal attempt to colonize Kentucky.

Boone's next major assignment was as a land agent for Henderson's Transylvania Land Company working to negotiate or trick the Shawnee Tribe into selling their lands. The goods promised in exchange for the lands were arranged to appear of much greater quantity and value than they actually possessed. For the meager sum of about $50,000 Henderson acquired a dubious title to all of what is now Kentucky, which he planned to make into the 14th colony with himself as its proprietor. There was much dissatisfaction about the compact among the tribes, and one chief gave an impassioned speech against the illegal private treaty:

> This is but the beginning. The invader has crossed the great sea in ships; he has not been stayed by broad rivers, and now he has penetrated the wilderness and overcome the ruggedness of the mountains. Neither will he stop here. He will force the Indian steadily before him across the Mississippi ever toward the west…till the red man be no longer roamer of the forests and a pursuer of wild game.[13]

Another chief remarked ominously to Boone at the conclusion of the treaty ceremony: "Brother, we have given you fine land, but I believe that you will have much trouble in settling it."[14]

In 1775 Henderson engaged Boone to carve out the "Wilderness Road" providing entrance to the "Great Grant" as it was euphemistically called. Boone's party of thirty "well-armed" axmen began the laborious work of cutting the road through the Cumberland Gap, again following ancient traces. The route of this early trail is known as "The Daniel Boone Heritage Trail." After completing the road Boone's party began building a settlement called Boonesborough consisting of a few crude fortified log cabins. Following an Indian raid Boone wrote to Henderson, asking for relief. The letter clearly reveals his motives:

> My brother and I went down and found two men killed and sculpted [scalped].… My advice to you, Sir, is to come or send [reinforcements] as soon as possible.… for the people are very uneasy, but are willing to stay and venture their lives with you; and now it the time to flusterate [frustrate] their [the Indians'] intentions and keep the country whilst we are in it. If we give way to them now, it will ever be the case.[15]

The uncertainties of the Revolutionary War period and the hostility of the Native Americans forestalled the land

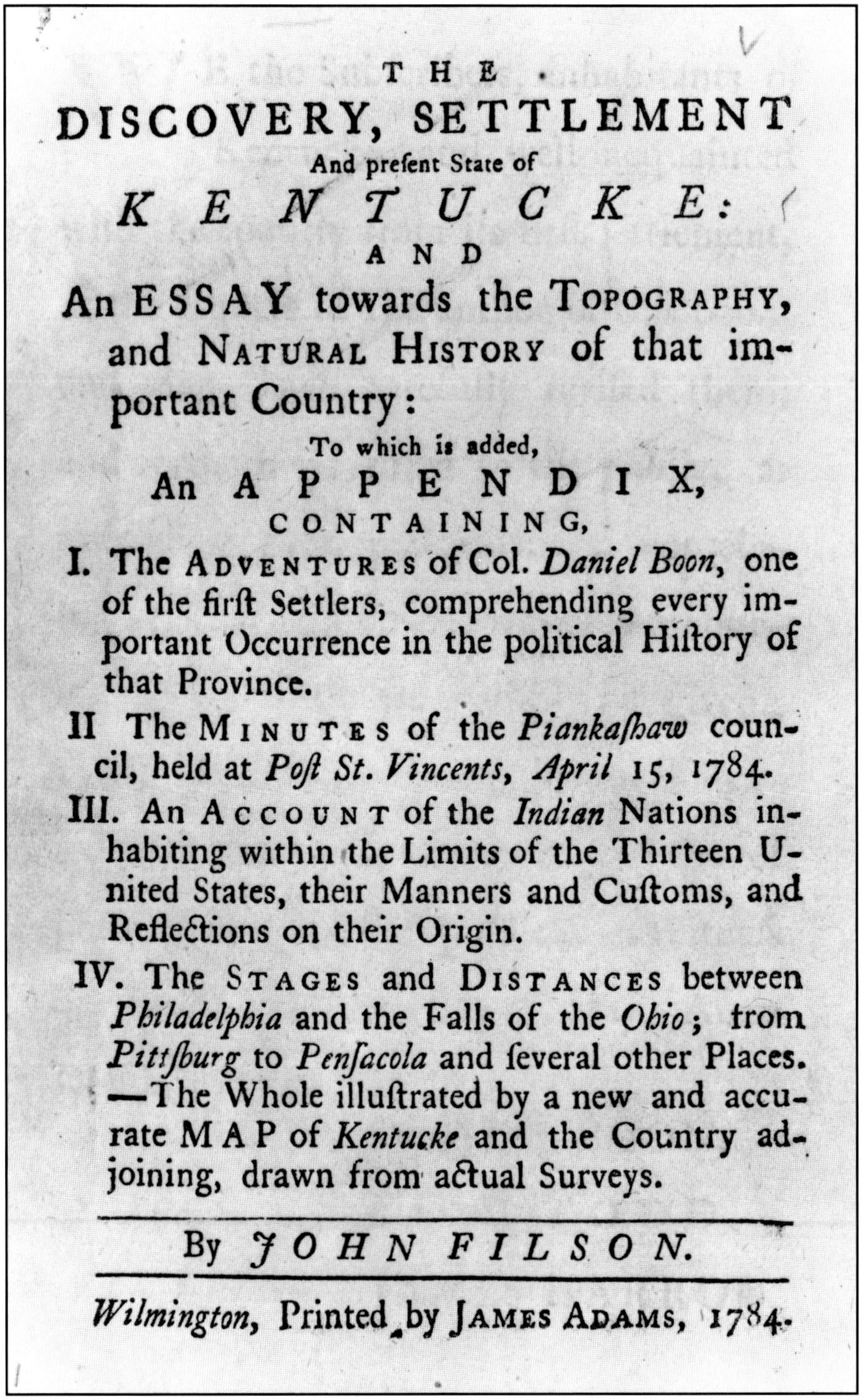

THE

DISCOVERY, SETTLEMENT

And prefent State of

KENTUCKE:

A N D

An ESSAY towards the TOPOGRAPHY, and NATURAL HISTORY of that important Country:

To which is added,

An APPENDIX,

C O N T A I N I N G,

I. The ADVENTURES of Col. *Daniel Boon*, one of the firſt Settlers, comprehending every important Occurrence in the political Hiſtory of that Province.

II The MINUTES of the *Piankaſhaw* council, held at *Poſt St. Vincents, April* 15, 1784.

III. An ACCOUNT of the *Indian* Nations inhabiting within the Limits of the Thirteen United States, their Manners and Cuſtoms, and Reflections on their Origin.

IV. The STAGES and DISTANCES between *Philadelphia* and the Falls of the *Ohio;* from *Pittſburg* to *Penſacola* and ſeveral other Places. —The Whole illuſtrated by a new and accurate MAP of *Kentucke* and the Country adjoining, drawn from actual Surveys.

By *JOHN FILSON.*

Wilmington, Printed by JAMES ADAMS, 1784.

Figure 1. Title page from John Filson's *The Discovery, Settlement And Present State of Kentucke,… To Which Is Added An Appendix, Containing "The Adventures of Daniel Boone."* (Wilmington, Del.: James Adams, 1784). George N. Meissner Collection, Special Collections, Olin Library, Washington University, St. Louis.

boom that Henderson and Boone had been promoting. The final blow to Henderson's Transylvania Company came when the Virginia Convention invalidated the company's "Great Grant" as lacking legislative authority. The decision ended the proprietary colony of Transylvania, and Boone lost his claim to thousands of acres in Kentucky.

During the years from 1776 to 1778, the British incited their Indian allies to attack the Americans on the Western frontier and Boonesborough suffered several raids by Indian forces. The most celebrated of these attacks was the brief abduction of Boone's daughter Jemima and her friends, the daughters of another settler, Richard Callaway. Their captivity was later sensationalized by Boone's mid-century biographers, although Filson allotted it only two sentences in his narrative. "On the fourteenth day of July, 1776, two of Col. Calaway's [sic] daughters, and one of mine, were taken prisoner near the fort. I immediately pursued the Indians, with only eight men, and on the sixteenth overtook them, killed two of the party, and recovered the girls."[16] The abduction became the subject of paintings by Carl Wimar and prints by Karl Bodmer in the early 1850s **(Figures 37, 38)**. James Fenimore Cooper also used the captivity of Boone's daughters as the basis for his popular novel of 1826, *The Last of the Mohicans*.[17] Cooper's main character in the Leatherstocking novels, Natty Bumppo, bears a striking resemblance to Daniel Boone.

In January 1778 Boone was captured by Shawnee tribesmen, and later his entire party surrendered to the natives. The group marched to Detroit, then a major British garrison in the West, where the Indians hoped to ransom the prisoners. During his captivity Boone was adopted by the tribe, and took up their dress and customs. Later, to explain the length of Boone's captivity and the ease with which he adapted to Indian life, a dark rumor circulated that Boone had betrayed his race and become a "white-Indian." This led to images of Boone's "Indian Toilette" **(Figure 2)** depicting him willingly assuming Indian ways. Filson's "autobiography" described Boone's adoption and escape:

> I was adopted, according to their custom, into a family, where I became a son, and had a great share of affection of my new parents, brothers, sisters and friends. I was exceedingly familiar and friendly with them, always appearing as cheerful and satisfied as possible, and they put great confidence in me. I often went hunting with them, and frequently gained their applause for my activity at our shooting matches.[18]

A few weeks later an Indian army arrived and laid protracted siege to Boonesborough, which had been reinforced, thanks to the warning provided by Boone's escape. Because of Boone's long absence in captivity, Rebecca Boone thought he was dead, and she returned to her family in North Carolina.

Boone's activities from the winter of 1778 through the fall of 1779 remain mysterious. Boone's statement, "The

Figure 2. *Boone's Indian Toilette.* Frontispiece in Cecil B. Hartley's *The Life of Daniel Boone: The Great Western Hunter and Pioneer.* (New York: Lovell, Coreyell and Co., no date). Charles W. Bryan, Jr. Collection, Special Collections, Olin Library, Washington University, St. Louis.

history of my going home, and returning with my family, forms a series of difficulties, an account of which would swell a volume, and being foreign to my purpose, I shall purposefully omit them," is surely disingenuous. It probably was intended to conceal trouble with the American authorities suspicious about the length of his stay with the Indians, and was an attempt to dispel rumors of secret double-dealing allegiances with the British, because of the Tory sympathies of his wife's family, the Bryans. He was accused of treason by Richard Callaway, and he was charged and tried by the American authorities. Although he was eventually vindicated of these suspicions, the ordeal left a psychological scar.

In the fall of 1779 Boone moved his family back to Boonesborough, which he found unbearable because of the suspicions about his loyalty. He moved on to erect a new

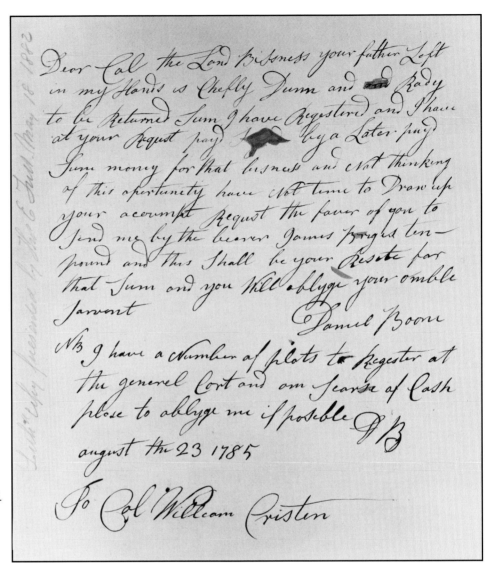

Letter from Daniel Boone to Col. William Cristen regarding his land business. August 23, 1785. The St. Louis Mercantile Library Association.

settlement called Boone's Station on one of his land claims. Soon after he sold these claims and set out for the capital of the Kentucky Territory in Williamsburg, Virginia, with about $50,000 of both his own and friends' money to purchase warrants for speculating on new tracts farther west. But misfortune struck again: he was robbed as he slept at an inn in James City, probably drugged by the innkeeper.[19] Boone was now destitute, and the loss of this fortune left him deeply depressed. Eventually he paid back all the funds that had been entrusted to him. Conflict with the natives continued and several of his relatives, including his brother Edward Boone, a brother-in-law William Bryan, and Richard Callaway (Jemima Boone's uncle) were killed in battle. At one point in 1780 Boone was taken prisoner by the British in Staunton, Virginia, but was eventually released by the British.

During 1782, called the "year of blood," the last great battles occurred between the Indian forces allied with the British and the American forces attempting to gain control of Kentucky and the Ohio River Valley. The Battle of Blue Licks, in which Boone's son Israel was killed, was a disastrous rout for the Americans, and the last major battle of the Revolutionary War, resulting in Boone's stoic comment, "Many widows were now made."[20]

The compelling reasons behind the intensity of the Native American attacks on Boone and the settlers he led has been preserved in a famous speech made by the "white-Indian" leader Simon Girty. It is an impassioned counterpart to the one-sided accounts of Boone's exploits against the Indians, and a legitimate expression of the natives' complaint against the settlers.

> *Brothers, the long knives [i.e. the Virginians] have overrun your country and usurped your hunting grounds. They have destroyed the cane, trodden down the clover, killed the deer and the buffalo, the beaver and the raccoon. The beaver has been chased from his dam, and forced to leave the country.*
>
> *Brothers: The intruders on your land exult in the success that has crowned their flagitious acts. They are*

planting fruit trees and plowing the lands where, not long since, were the canebreak and the clover field.... Unless you rise in the majesty of your might and exterminate their whole race, you may bid adieu to the hunting grounds of your fathers—to the delicious flesh of the animals with which they once abounded—and to the skins with which you were once enabled to purchase your clothing and rum.[21]

Following the War of Revolution the Boone family moved to Limestone, Kentucky, where Daniel set up a store and tavern and entered further into the lucrative business of land surveying. The store and tavern prospered, especially from the sale of liquor to Indians and settlers, although Boone's business of land surveying turned out to be his financial downfall. His surveys were sometimes wildly imprecise, leading to "shingled" or overlapping claims. His greatest problem, however, seems to have been his failure to master the complex legal process of land registration. This was perhaps the most prosperous period of his life, although eventually he was left bankrupt by a series of ruinous lawsuits. Boone's baffling blend of ambition and self-denial was essential to understanding the paradox of his personality, and his own seeming inability to adapt to the very civilization he was bringing to the West. The paradox and failure implicit in his personality became most apparent during his last decade in Kentucky. Repeated disappointment in business and politics resulted in his withdrawal by migrating farther westward into the wilderness. Rather than oppose the legal challenges against his land claims, Boone left Kentucky for Missouri where he could reestablish a freehold affirmed by the rifle, not by law.

By the mid-1790s Boone had become famous as a result of the publication of Filson's *Kentucke*, which was widely reprinted. In 1799 he decided to leave Kentucky for St. Charles County, Missouri, where his son had already settled. He was more than sixty years old and again he was moving west. In his 1827 novel *The Prairie* James Fenimore Cooper described the event as "the elders" of Ohio and Kentucky leading their descendants deeper into the West "in quest of that which might be termed, without the aid of poetry, their natural and more congenial atmosphere." Cooper averred, "The distinguished and resolute forester who first penetrated the wilds of [Kentucky], was of the number. This adventurous and venerable patriarch was now seen making his last remove...."[22] In a note Cooper makes the connection certain, identifying the figure as "Colonel Boone, the patriarch of Kentucky. This venerable and hardy pioneer of civilization emigrated to an estate three hundred miles west of the Mississippi, in his ninety-second year [he was about sixty], because he found a population of ten to the square mile inconveniently crowded!"[23]

In Missouri, Boone's fame as land promoter was reasserted when he was offered land by the Spanish governors of the Louisiana Territory in exchange for inducing other settlers to come to Missouri. Such was the renown of his name that settlers came to Missouri. In payment Boone received a large grant from the Spanish, most of which he lost because of claims against him from his faulty surveys in Kentucky. In 1810, while traveling on the Ohio River to visit his brother Squire, he met John James Audubon. Audubon reputedly painted a portrait of Boone, although this is no longer extant, and he wrote the following account of hunting with the famous marksman Boone.

Barking off squirrels is delightful sport, and in my opinion requires a greater degree of accuracy than any other. I first witnessed this manner of procuring squirrels whilst near the town of Frankfort. The performer was the celebrated Daniel Boon.... My companion, a stout, hale, and athletic man, dressed in homespun hunting-shirt, bare-legged and moccasined, carried a long and heavy rifle, which, as he was loading it, he said had proved efficient in all his former undertakings, and which he hoped would not fail on this occasion, as he felt proud to show me his skill.... Boon kept up his firing, and before many hours had elapsed, we had procured as many squirrels as we wished....[24]

In 1813 Rebecca, Boone's wife of fifty-six years, died, and shortly after a manuscript autobiography was lost by his old friend Flanders Callaway, and Boone was by then too old, he claimed, to attempt to reconstruct it. About 1816 he is said to have made his last hunting expedition at the age of eighty-two. He traveled up the Missouri to the site of Kansas City, and perhaps went as far as the Yellowstone. The last major account of Boone was made by the itinerant portrait painter Chester Harding, who sought out Boone in 1820, and left a lengthy report recounting his creation of the first painting of Daniel Boone **(Color Plate 1, Figures 3, 5, 6)**. According to the modern historian John Bakeless, Harding neglected to mention that Boone was so old and ill that he could not hold his head still, and a friend had to stand behind him and hold his head steady while the artist worked.[25] He was buried in a simple grave near his wife Rebecca.

In 1845 the last act of Daniel Boone's many migrations was played out when the Frankfort Cemetery Company decided to capitalize on the fame of the pioneer. Officials from the Frankfort Cemetery Company appealed to Boone's family to remove Boone's remains to Frankfort. A grand celebration complete with a parade and marching band greeted in fine style the mortal remains of Lieutenant-Colonel Daniel Boone of the Kentucky militia. His bones and those of Rebecca, or what little of them could be identified, were ceremoniously placed in a vault with speeches and declarations extolling his many contributions to opening the state. Around 1856 Joseph R. Meeker painted the *Graves of Daniel Boone and His Wife* in the cemetery at Frankfort "overshadowed by several noble trees," which was raffled by the Cosmopolitan Art Association. Unfortunately, Meeker's painting is no longer extant.[26] The promised monument was finally constructed in 1862.

Figure 3. Chester Harding, *Daniel Boone*. 1820.
Oil on canvas, 29" x 24". Private Collection.

CHAPTER II

Creating a Hero:
John Filson's *Kentucke* and Chester Harding's *Life Portrait*

The reality of Daniel Boone was that he was hardly the ideal, heroic figure that his biographers and later hagiographers constructed in the numerous texts about him that flooded the American and European book market following the appearance of John Filson's *Kentucke* in 1784 **(Figure 1)**. These texts provided the material for the fabrications that became the popular legend of Daniel Boone through the 19th century, a heroic persona composed of fiction and fact, not much resembling the man described in the preceding chapter. Filson's Boone was in essence a figure at the crux of complex cultural and economic considerations. An account of the interpretive "spins" on the story of Daniel Boone beginning with John Filson's seminal book is essential to understanding the various ideological inventions that underlay the visual images of Boone that are the subject of this exhibition.

In 1784 John Filson returned from two years in Kentucky where he worked as a land surveyor and speculator, and had come to know Boone well. Filson and Boone and several other men had formed a partnership to develop land along the Ohio, and since Filson was the most literate of the group he became the publicist for the company. In Wilmington he quickly got up a short book entitled *The Discovery, Settlement And Present State of Kentucke*. Importantly, the first chapter added the word "Purchase" to Filson's main title. Filson's *Kentucke* was essentially little more than an elaborate real estate promotion designed to advertise the West to Easterners and Europeans. Filson's book was similar in approach to Thomas Jefferson's *Notes on the State of Virginia* that appeared the following year. Filson's basic problem was that the market for Western land was weak because the Revolution had just ended, and the fierce Indian wars that had ravaged the fledgling settlements in Kentucky were unnerving potential buyers. Filson needed a hero figure—a champion—who could reassure his readers that emigration was practical and who would extol the promise of the frontier, without unduly understating the very real dangers of buying land in the West.

The promotional nature of Filson's book was candidly acknowledged in the "Preface" in which the author at-

tempted to preserve his integrity by protesting his impartiality, perhaps a little too forcefully.

When I visited Kentucke, I found it so far to exceed my expectations, although great, that I concluded it was a pity, that the world had not adequate information of it. I conceived that a proper description, and map of it, were objects highly interesting to the United States; and therefore, incredible as it may appear to some, I must declare, that this performance is not published from lucrative motives, but solely to inform the world of the happy climate, and plentiful soil of this favored region.[27]

Filson informed readers that his book would afford "much advantage" to its possessor as it was a "Compleat Guide." His veracity was attested to by the testimonial of "Col. Boon, Col. Todd, and Col. Harrod" who had "chearfully contributed with a disinterested view of being servicable to the public."[28] In effect Boone was simply a shill for the land developers that he and Filson represented, and his "autobiography" was finally nothing more than a dramatization of his desire to sell the wilderness by presenting himself in a brazen self-promotion as the originator of an emerging imperial republic.

As Filson reconstructed him, Daniel Boone was transformed from a simple folk hero into a far grander being. From the outset Boone's figure was cleverly commodified in Filson's account in order to benefit the interests of his partners in land speculation. The frontiersman Boone, as purveyed by the astute Filson, represented one of the earliest examples of a new type of American hero. Filson's Boone unhesitatingly stated that he was "an instrument ordained [by Providence] to settle the wilderness."[29] The shrewd Presbyterian Filson merged the Puritan trope of a sacred mission in the wilderness with the idea of divine intervention in human affairs manifested through an individual like Boone. From the opening lines of Boone's "autobiography" this key idea is apparent:

Let those influencing power actuate, but the permission or disposal of Providence, from selfish or social views, yet in time the mysterious will of Heaven is unfolded, and

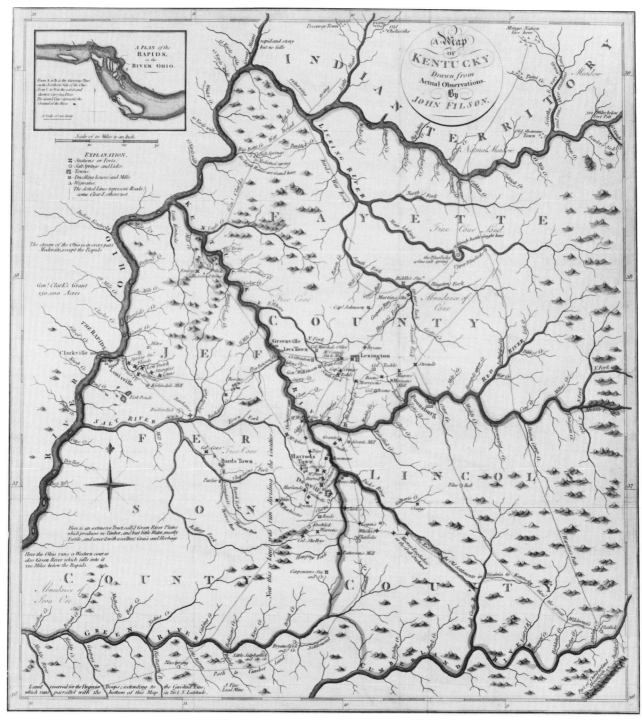

Figure 4. *Map of Kentucke*. In the English edition of John Filson's *Kentucke*. (Picadilly: John Stockdate, 1793). Charles W. Bryan, Jr. Collection, Special Collections, Olin Library, Washington University, St. Louis.

*we behold our conduct, from what-soever motives excited,
operating to answer the important designs of heaven. Thus
we behold Kentucky, lately a howling wilderness, the
habitation of savages and wild beasts, become a fruitful
field; this region, so favorably distinguished by nature, now
become the habitation of civilization, at a period unparal-
leled in history, in the midst of a raging war, and under all
the disadvantages of emigration to a country so remote
from the inhabited parts of the continent. Here where the
hand of violence shed the blood of the innocent; where the
horrid yells of savages, and the groans of the distressed,
founded in our ears, we now hear the praises and adora-
tions of our Creator; where wretched wigwams stood, the
miserable abodes of savages, we behold the foundations of
cities laid, that, in all probability, will rival the glory of the
greatest upon earth.*[30]

Filson's assertion that Boone acted as an instrument of
Providence "operating to answer the important designs of
heaven" was in essence a forerunner of the typological
conception of the hero whose acts simultaneously serve
personal, national and divine purposes. Such a heroic figure
had the nearly supernatural power to justify "selfish or social"
motives at the same time appearing to advance larger
national objectives like the establishment of great cities in a
transcontinental empire that would "rival the glory of the
greatest upon the earth." Filson's creation of Boone as
instrument of progress was to be one of the most enduring
contributions of his slender volume.

The structure of Filson's *Kentucke*, as Slotkin has
observed, is modeled on the format of a Puritan sermon,
almost like one of the famed Jeremiads, or political sermons
of the New England Puritans. In those sermons the exhorta-
tion to moral and social improvement to overcome a world
of woe is often linked with the coming of a millennial age
following a divine struggle to settle land that Providence has
promised His chosen people. But where the traditional
sermon began with a biblical text, Slotkin notes, "Filson
takes a map of Kentucky for his text. His plan is to develop
the meaning inherent in the land in much the same way
that the Puritan sermon exfoliates the meaning in the
biblical passage."[31] It is no coincidence that Filson's map is
watermarked with the words "Work & be Rich" and with a
plowshare **(Figure 4)**.

Filson's *Kentucke* abounds with imagistic evocations of
the beckoning beauty and fertility of the landscape, which
Boone called a "second paradise." In such a place it was
impossible to be "disposed to melancholy." "No populous
city," Boone declared, "with all the varieties of commerce
and stately structures, could afford so much pleasure to my
mind, as the beauties of nature I found here."[32] The richness
of the land and its potential for agriculture seemed unlimited, but the creation of this agrarian utopia required
suffering and sacrifice in a Holy War with the racially

inferior savage Indians. Despite the settlers' tribulations with
Indians the outcome is inevitable: "What thanks, what
ardent and ceaseless thanks are due to that all-superintend-
ing Providence which has turned a cruel war into peace,
brought order out of confusion, made the fierce savages
placid, and turned away their hostile weapons from our
country!"[33]

The astonishing importance of Boone for 19th-century
Americans was thus carefully fabricated by Filson to corre-
spond perfectly with the cultural and ideological needs of a
nation eager to annex its new empire in the West. Boone
was the ideal hero figure for the new nation: a common man
through which divine will operated. Boone's heroic deeds
made him an ideal model for other settlers, but he was not a
divinity and certainly not an aristocrat. Boone symbolized
through all his actions the appealing idea of a glorious
national destiny open to everyman that lay in the future and
on the Western frontier.

In actuality, Boone's career embodied an exploitative
ideology of colonization in which the land was claimed on
paper and perhaps only superficially improved, its value
quickly increased by speculation, while the Indian was to be
"saved" by the appropriation of his lands, protected from the
contaminating influence of civilization by removal to
remote, unwanted lands further west, or, if necessary,
exterminated. Progress, as this process was known, was
sanctioned by the self-serving desire to believe that Divine
Providence manifested its grand plan of history through
heroic men like Boone who had been ordained to create the
new American empire. Understanding what Boone symbolized clarifies how the figure created by Filson, and other
writers, could so fascinate Americans during the Jacksonian
period and into the 1860s.

The extraordinary usefulness of Filson's text to the
backers of westward expansion, largely land speculators and a
new-money class of Eastern entrepreneurs willing to finance
Western settlement, is attested to by the numerous editions
and variations that were published after the first edition, and
that continued unabated into the 1850s. Boone's fictional
persona—the smaller part based on fact and the larger part
embellished if not invented by Filson—was ultimately
addressed to an urban market in the cities of the East and in
Europe. During the early-19th century the demand for cheap
land in the West was growing because of a swelling population of emigrants. In order to reach the desired "upscale"
market of settlers Filson cleverly portrayed Boone as a forest
philosopher, a kind of republican stoic, a man of thought and
poetic reflection, as well as a man of daring action and
indomitable courage. *Kentucke*, with Boone as its protagonist, was virtually unprecedented in American literature for
one reason: Filson primarily addressed his book to a national
audience. Filson even sought George Washington's endorse-
ment for a second edition, but Washington declined.[34]

Despite Boone's growing popularity in the late-18th and

Figure 5. Chester Harding, *Daniel Boone*. 1820. Oil on canvas, 21 1/2" x 16 1/2". Collection of the Massachusetts Historical Society, Boston. Gift of George T. Bigelow.

Figure 6. Chester Harding, *Daniel Boone*. 1820. Oil on oilcloth remounted on canvas, 23 1/2 "x 19". Private Collection.

early-19th century it was not until the very end of the old frontiersman's life around 1820 that an American artist first grasped the potential profits to be gained from painting his portrait **(Figure 5)**. The period following the War of 1812 witnessed a renewed interest in expansion into the Ohio and Mississippi River Valleys, and the American public was increasingly aware of the frontiersman as a special kind of American champion. To be sure, during the 1820s and 1830s American artists were slow to realize the historic importance and commercial potential of depicting the movement westward that had begun with Boone and his comrades during the Revolutionary War.

In 1820 the aspiring itinerant portrait painter Chester Harding (1792-1866) was only beginning his career. After visiting his brother Horace Harding in Paris, Kentucky, he toured cities along the Ohio River including Cincinnati, and found himself in St. Louis. Harding, like so many artists of his day, had begun his career as a house painter and moved up to the honorable trade of painting well-to-do sitters in provincial Western cities. But in the depths of the financial crisis of 1820, following the Panic of 1819, this work offered so little income that the artist, following the urging of Governor William Clark of Missouri, decided to seek out the old man Daniel Boone and paint his portrait. Whether Harding may have read accounts of Boone's life is unknown, although it appears that profit, not literary inspiration, motivated him. He left St. Louis in June 1820 for the Femme Osage Valley in St. Charles County, Missouri, to find the aged pioneer. Harding described in some detail his experience in his autobiography, *My Egotistigraphy*:

> *In June of this year I made a trip of one hundred miles for the purpose of painting the portrait of old Colonel Daniel Boone. I had much trouble in finding him. He was living, some miles from the main road, in one of the cabins of an old block-house which was built for the protection of the settlers against the incursion of the Indians. I found that the nearer I got to his dwelling, the less was known of him. When within two miles of his house, I asked a man to tell me where Colonel Boone lived. He said he did not know any such man. "Why, yes, you do," said his wife. "It is that white-headed old man who lives on the bottom, near the river." A good illustration of the proverb, that a prophet is not without honor save in his own country.[35]*

As Leah Lipton has explained in her article on Harding's portraits of Boone, there are at least eight extant versions of the Boone portrait. Thanks to Lipton's research, it is now possible to ascertain which of these is the portrait that Harding completed of Boone in 1820, and which are later versions or replicas. Harding's account of his discovery and painting of Boone provides valuable documentation about the character of the old Kentuckian at the end of his life. According to the artist:

I found the object of my search engaged in cooking his dinner. He was lying on his bunk, near the fire, and had a long strip of venison wound round his ramrod, and was busy turning it before a brisk blaze, and using salt and pepper to season his meat. I at once told him the object of my visit. I found he hardly knew what I meant. I explained the matter to him, and he agreed to sit. He was ninety years old [he was actually eighty-six], and rather infirm; his memory of passing events was much impaired, yet he would amuse me every day by his anecdotes of his earlier life. I asked him one day, just after his description of one of his long hunts, if he ever got lost, having no compass. "No," said he, "I can't say as ever I was lost, but I was bewildered once for three days."

He was much astonished at seeing the likeness. He had a very large progeny; one granddaughter had eighteen children, all at home near the old man's cabin; they were even more astonished at the picture than the old man himself.[36]

While Boone was sitting for him, Harding made a pencil sketch, now lost, and a small oil study on canvas **(Figure 5)**. During the summer of 1820 in the leisure of his studio in Franklin, Missouri, Harding produced at least two finished portraits of Daniel Boone employing the pencil and oil sketches as the sources for both portraits. One was a half-length figure wearing a brown coat with a dark fur collar, a red waistcoat, and a metal knife holder attached to a brown leather belt **(Color Plate 1, Figure 3)**, while the other was a full-length portrait, painted on a table oilcloth.[37] During this brief stay in Franklin the creation of these replicas by Harding was witnessed by nine-year-old George Caleb Bingham—an event that left an indelible impression on Bingham's mind.[38] Harding's ambitious full-length painting of Boone was nearly destroyed after the artist loaned it to the Kentucky State Capitol hoping that the legislature would purchase it. He finally retrieved the picture in the fall of 1861 and found it "banged about until the greater part of it was broken to pieces.... The head is as perfect as when it was painted, in color, though there are some small almost imperceptible cracks in it."[39] Harding cut out the undamaged head and fastened the piece of oil cloth to a new canvas, and hired another painter to complete the background. As Lipton observes, the painting exists today in this curious composite form, with the attached oil cloth on canvas plainly evident **(Figure 6)**. This lost full-length portrait was, however, to be of special importance in depictions of Boone by later artists.

The appearance of Harding's lost full-length portrait of Boone can be reconstructed from an engraving produced by the self-taught St. Louis artist, James Otto Lewis (1799-1858) **(Figure 7)**.[40] Within a few weeks of Boone's death on September 26, 1820 advertisements appeared in *The St. Louis Enquirer* and *The Missouri Republican* offering subscriptions to Lewis's engraving after Harding's painting.

Harding and Lewis (Adv.)
Proposals for publishing, by subscription, an engraving of the venerable Daniel Boone.
Conditions: The size of the print will be 15" x 10". Engraved full length from a characteristic and correct painting on paper of first quality. The price to subscribers will be $3.00 payable on delivery. Subscriptions will be received by James O. Lewis, Engraver, St. Louis.[41]

The *Missouri Gazette and Public Advertiser* of St. Louis carried the same notice and added the following patriotic enticement to potential purchasers of the Harding-Lewis print.

To transmit to the posterity of a country the actions and features of those who fought and bled in her cause is a duty too sacred and useful to neglect. While the memory of the heroic deeds of the early adventures is passing away, this work will be the means of rescuing from oblivion the features of one who took the most active part in sustaining the early settlements of the Western country.[42]

Leah Lipton notes that Harding often capitalized on opportunities to sell editions of engravings of his famous sitters. Eventually all the engravings were sold, although today only two prints from the suite can be located, one, exhibited and reproduced here, from the St. Louis Art Museum and the other at the Missouri Historical Society.

A later variation on Harding's full-length portrait of Boone was completed by James B. Longacre for his *National Portrait Gallery of Distinguished Americans* **(Figure 9)**. Lipton observes that the source for this engraving was the painting of Boone with a fur collar coat, now in a private collection **(Figure 3)**. This painting was also the source for Longacre's small sepia wash drawing after Harding's full-length portrait **(Figure 8)**.

From an iconographic perspective both Harding portraits and the variations created after them by Longacre are significant. They can be related to a group of portraits of prominent individuals in fur-collar coats. "The prototype for these portraits was Allan Ramsay's portrait of Jean Jacques Rousseau in a fur cap and fur collar," according to Dawn Glanz, which was followed by several portraits of Benjamin Franklin wearing a coat with a fur collar or his famous Canadian fur hat.[43] Certainly Harding could have seen Rembrandt Peale's 1805 portrait of Thomas Jefferson **(Figure 10)** during his visit to Philadelphia in 1819-1820 to study art at the Pennsylvania Academy of the Fine Arts, just before he traveled to Missouri to paint Boone.[44]

The fur trimmed collar was thus a symbol of status unique to the new democratic society. According to Glanz, Harding's appropriation of the motif for his portrait of Boone significantly expanded the iconographic tradition. In transferring the fur-collar coat to Boone, Harding symbolically elevated him to the status of Franklin and Jefferson as a Western or frontier representative of the illustrious statesman or philosopher, and "also as a perfect representative of Rousseau's 'natural man.'"[45] Interestingly, in the Harding/Lewis engraving the fur collar has been replaced by buckskin fringes, a symbol that would in time come to be even more closely associated with the West, as symbolized by the mountain man, fur trader and scout.

Notably, however, Boone's status in the emerging pantheon of American heroes differed from that of Franklin and Jefferson in several important ways. The hunting knife displayed in Boone's belt alludes to the fact that, unlike literary or scientific *philosophes* such as Rousseau, Diderot, Franklin, or Jefferson, Boone is the offspring of the American wilderness. This key detail implies that as a child of nature he is on familiar terms with the wilderness and considers it a resource to be exploited and, if necessary, an adversary to be conquered by violent means.

In that respect, the Kentucky long rifle is a master symbol in both the Harding/Lewis engraving and in Longacre's drawing, and in almost every subsequent painting and print depicting the pathfinder. Although most long rifles were made in Pennsylvania, their fame quickly spread because of their part in the conquest of Kentucky by Boone and others.[46] The fame of the long rifle further increased because of its role in the War of 1812, when Andrew Jackson's troops—many of whom were drawn from Kentucky and Tennessee—used it with deadly effectiveness at the Battle of New Orleans. In the Harding/Lewis engraving the weapon is prominent in the composition forming one side of the triangular form, the apex of which is Boone's head.

A third attribute introduced in the Harding/Lewis engraving, and probably also present in Harding's lost full length painting, is the hunting dog at Daniel Boone's feet. It would be easy to underestimate the value and importance of domesticated hunting dogs for pioneers moving westward, and in fact the dog appears in every major image of Boone from Cole to Ranney to Bingham.[47] In the Harding/Lewis print the alert animal is small and flop-eared, evidently on guard even as his master relaxes for his portrait.

The wilderness background in Harding and Lewis's print is also significant. Boone is posed against a large, solid tree with leaves that suggest the rugged oak. One large branch at

Figure 7. James Otto Lewis (after Chester Harding), *Daniel Boone*. 1820. Stipple engraving, 11 3/4" x 8 1/8" (sheet size). The Saint Louis Art Museum, Museum Purchase.

Figure 8. James B. Longacre (after Chester Harding), *Daniel Boone*. c. 1834. Sepia wash on cardboard, 2 1/4" x 2" (image size), 3 1/4" x 3 5/8" (sheet size). The New-York Historical Society.

Figure 9. James B. Longacre (after Chester Harding), *Daniel Boone.* 1835. Line and stipple engraving, 4 5/16" x 3 5/8 ". In James Herring and James B. Longacre, *National Portrait Gallery of Distinguished Americans*, Vol. 2. (Philadelphia: H. Perkins, 1835). The St. Louis Mercantile Library Association.

Figure 10. Rembrandt Peale, *Thomas Jefferson.* 1805. Oil on canvas, 28" x 23 1/2". The New-York Historical Society.

right has been broken off and lies at the pathfinder's feet. Beneath the broken branch is a log that bears the marks of being cut by an ax, subtly reinforcing the idea that where Boone goes nature must yield.

Harding must have hoped that the State of Kentucky would acquire the painting as an "official" memorial to Boone's role in opening the state to settlement, especially following the removal of Boone's remains from Missouri for reburial in Kentucky in 1845. On February 10, 1848, *The Daily Commonwealth* in Frankfort carried an unsigned letter reiterating Harding's offer to sell his Boone portrait to the State of Kentucky.

Mr. Editor: Are the members of the legislature aware that the portrait of Daniel Boone — pioneer of Kentucky

— which is now in the Governor's office is about to be removed from the state by Mr. Harding, the painter of it?

This is the only painting of the old hunter ever taken from life, and Kentucky should never permit it to go. $200 will keep it. If the legislature will not vote the money to buy it, will not each member subscribe $1 toward the object? The balance could be easily raised.

Mr. Harding has been offered $500 for this portrait by a historical society of Boston — but having once offered it to Kentucky for $200 he still gives her a chance to keep it.[48]

The appeal was in vain, however, because by then the State of Kentucky had acquired a different Boone portrait for the Capitol by William C. Allan.

Figure 11. Thomas Cole, *Daniel Boone at His Cabin at Great Osage Lake*. 1826.
Oil on canvas, 38" x 42 1/2". Mead Art Museum, Amherst College, Massachusetts.

CHAPTER III

A Hermit in Buckskins:
Thomas Cole's *Daniel Boone at His Cabin at Great Osage Lake*

After the American victory in the War of 1812 the growing power of Westerners who had played a major role in the war was increasingly disturbing to conservative Federalists in the Northeast. They feared disruption of the established social order by the growing demands of Westerners for political enfranchisement and social equality. Thus, in such traditional quarters, Boone was viewed not as a hero, but as a dangerous embodiment of Western tendencies toward democratic radicalism. There were also apprehensions that men like Boone living in the wilderness might adopt Indian customs leading to possible racial degeneracy, and, even worse, reversion to white-Indian renegades.

Among such wealthy classes the heroic persona that Filson had created certainly was not yet considered a desirable subject for a work of fine art. Eastern painters like Thomas Cole and writers like Daniel Bryan and C. Wilder responded by endowing Boone's image with a contradictory mixture of superficial social graces and Western primitivism. In creating this ambiguous representation of Boone they satisfied their well-to-do patrons by representing the frontiersman as uncontrollable and primitive, and yet they simultaneously appealed to Eastern curiosity about the little-known backwoodsmen of the West.

In 1813 Daniel Bryan, Boone's nephew, published his epic poem *The Mountain Muse: Comprising the Adventures of Daniel Boone and the Power of Virtuous and Refined Beauty* **(Figure 12)**, perhaps the most implausible of all the texts derived from Filson's *Kentucke*. Bryan further exaggerated the lofty style of his source, but Bryan, a former Tory, added a new idea because he transformed Boone into an aristocrat in buckskins. Bryan's poem was distorted by his desire to write an American epic in the grand manner of Milton and Scott, and by the intrinsic limitations of his subject—the frontier exploits of his uncle.

In Bryan's poem Filson's real estate promotion was transformed, albeit ineptly, into sentimental verse. Take for example the celebrated incident where Boone ascended the "commanding ridge" to survey the future wealth of Kentucky. Bryan described it this way:

Swift on, o'er the rude-featured Wilderness
The sinewy sons of Enterprise proceed.
Lo! now the farthest mountain-ledge they scale,
And from its breezy summit raptured see,
Kentucky's rolling Hills and broad Campaigns [sic]!
Prophetic transports thrill'd their kindling hearts,
Unwanted ebullitions warm'd their blood,
And God's Omnipotence and Wisdom waked
Profoundest adoration of their souls;
As in continued prospect they beheld
Green-mantled Groves and blossom-tinted Knolls,
Of their wide-ranging Vision, and survey'd
Through prescient Fancy's telescopic tube,
Republic-institutions rising round
The rich Expanse, beneath the angelic aid,
Of Conquest-crown'd Columbian Liberty.[49]

Bryan struggled to convert Boone into a Romantic hero symbolizing the idea of the frontiersman as a representative of upper-class American virtues, elaborated upon with a ludicrous degree of rhetorical embellishment. Understandably, Bryan's poem had little perceptible influence in promulgating the Boone mystique because Westerners wanted realism, not poetic license, and Easterners found the subject inherently distasteful. Boone himself was so annoyed with the pretentiousness of Bryan's poem that he remarked that he would have sued for slander had not the author been a relative. In understated frontier humor he observed that such works "ought to be left until the person was put into the ground."[50]

The most notable literary manifestation of uncertainty about Boone's persona as a symbol of civilization on the Western frontier was the bowdlerized edition of Filson published by C. Wilder in Brooklyn in 1823, entitled *The Life and Adventures of Colonel Daniel Boone . . . .*[51] Wilder's text found immediate application in a picture of Boone by the ambitious young painter Thomas Cole. Cole translated virtually intact motifs from Wilder into his painting of Boone reposing in front of his cabin in the wilderness. The result was an ambiguous depiction of Boone, but one in which image and text disclose striking similarities.

Cole's *Daniel Boone at His Cabin at Great Osage Lake* **(Color Plate 2, Figure 11)**, painted in 1826, is a romantic representation of the famous Kentuckian who had been dead only six years when Cole began the work. The painting was reproduced in *The Token*, where the editor described it as "a fancy piece."[52] The term "fancy piece" denoted the idea of artistic invention or fantasy. In Cole's case, fancy meant the subtle representation of his conservative social views.[53]

Cole found in Wilder's book a conception of Boone entirely sympathetic with his own disapproval of Westerners and common men in general. Cole was suspicious of egalitarian political trends emerging in the mid-1820s that demanded a more democratic society.[54] Many upper-class Easterners, especially those of the conservative or Federalist political persuasion, feared the increasing political power of the lower classes. Frontiersmen, symbolized by Boone, were equated with these dangerous democratic tendencies, and

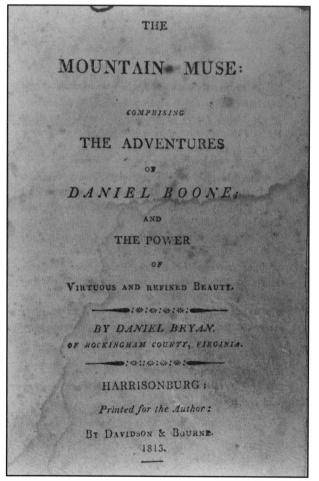

Figure 12. Title page from Daniel Bryan, *The Mountain Muse: Comprising the Adventures of Daniel Boone and the Power of Virtuous and Refined Beauty.* (Harrisonburg: Davidson and Bourne, 1813). George N. Meissner Collection, Special Collections, Olin Library, Washington University, St. Louis.

their assertion of new-found political authority in the states they created were a particular threat to established power. The egalitarian "Western" tendencies that concerned Cole and his conservative patrons were symbolized by the election of the Western Democrat Andrew Jackson only three years later.

Furthermore, the English-born Cole followed Wilder's concept and worried about the subversion of traditional social values because of the temptation of Indian customs. The acquisition of Cole's painting of Boone by Samuel Griswold Goodrich, the editor of *The Token*, was, therefore, a telling indication that Cole's conception was acceptable to the elite social classes Cole hoped to attract as patrons. From Cole's perspective Goodrich was an ideal patron. Goodrich and his family were members of the New England aristocracy, and in his youth he had moved in the highest social circles.[55]

Cole must have found in Wilder's text a view of Boone that was completely sympathetic with his own conservative position. Key passages were translated directly into his picture as the artist took Wilder's text as the program for his painting. Wilder spoke mockingly of Boone's "prejudice" in favor of the Indians and his dislike of "D—-d Yankees." Wilder's comment on Boone's regard for Indians must have been especially meaningful to the artist.

> *By the foregoing the reader will perceive how greatly prejudiced was Colonel Boone in favor of the tawny inhabitants of the Western wilderness [Indians], whose manners and habits he did not hesitate to declare to the day of this death were far more agreeable to him than those of a more civilized and refined race.*[56]

The notion that Boone found the manners and habits of Indians more agreeable than those of "a more civilized and refined [white] race" was appealing to Cole as he grappled with the problem of how to represent the frontiersman. Careful study of the preparatory drawing for the painting **(Figure 13)** discloses that the body of Boone was overlaid by the artist on an earlier drawing of an Indian figure. This Indian appears in Cole's painting *Solitary Lake, New Hampshire* **(Figure 14)**. The bodies of the Indian and Boone are virtually identical except for their heads and Boone's upraised arm holding his rifle. To complete the figure of Boone in the painting the head of an old man at the upper left in the drawing was joined to the body of Boone that covers the Indian figure. The superimposition of the hunter Boone over an Indian hunter is of great importance, because it is evidence of Cole's acceptance of Wilder's allegations that Boone had all but abandoned white civilization to take up Indian ways. Discerning the underlying process of conceptual development in the preliminary drawing is essential to decoding Cole's painting. Another unusual aspect of Cole's personification of Boone is that, unlike all later depictions of the pathfinder, Cole's Boone is scowling.

Figure 13. Thomas Cole, *Sketch for Daniel Boone Sitting at the Door of His Cabin.* c. 1825-1826.
Pencil, pen, and wash on paper, 9 3/8" x 8 1/2". Mead Art Museum, Amherst College, Massachusetts. Museum Purchase.

Figure 14. Detail,Thomas Cole, *Solitary Lake, New Hampshire*. Olana Historic Site, New York Office of Parks, Recreation and Historic Preservation.

His gaze is far from friendly or inviting. The preparatory drawing again reveals the process by which Cole created this unsociable expression. On the drawing, an isolated head of a bald-headed old man, probably sketched from life, is rendered at the upper left.[57] Below this head are several faint sketches of faces with grimacing expressions, examples of various presentations of anger probably derived from drawing manuals or perhaps books about phrenology. The scowling expression in the sketchy face just below the completed head seems to have been adapted for the final model of Boone's face.

The unfriendly gaze that Cole creates for his Boone was based on an assertion in Wilder's text that in order to pursue his frontier life without restraint, "the great object of the Colonel appears to have been to live as far as possible from every white inhabitant."[58] Furthermore, "he [Boone] (like the unrefined Savage) viewed the rapid increase of population with more distrust than satisfaction."[59] According to Wilder,

> It was frequently remarked by him, that while he could never with safety repose confidence in a Yankee, he had never been deceived by an Indian, when he had once declared himself friendly disposed; and that so far as his own experience would enable him to judge, he would certainly prefer a state of nature to a state of civilization.[60]

As Cole constructed his image of Boone through reading Wilder, such passages must have possessed signifi-

cance for the young artist. Only a few years earlier the artist had experienced extreme hardship wandering the Ohio River frontier in a frustrating search for patrons who could appreciate his conviction that he had been given a higher calling in art.[61]

Perhaps the most unusual feature of Cole's Boone is that underneath his buckskin jacket he wears rumpled purple leggings. What meaning might these unusual clothes possess? Nowhere in Wilder's text is there any precedent for this curious feature of Boone's dress. Traditionally the color purple is associated with royalty, and perhaps Boone's purple leggings are meant to suggest that underneath Boone's rough exterior he was also a distinguished figure—the lord of his wilderness domain—who rebuffs with his fierce gaze unwelcome settlement. Such symbolism is, of course, partially contradictory to another of Cole's underlying ideas that Boone is simultaneously a white man gone primitive, become almost a dreaded white-Indian.

According to Wilder, Boone rejected civilization when the frontiersman saw smoke rising along the horizon from other settlers' cabins. It was then that he knew it was time to move farther west to escape the contaminating influence of advancing civilization. Wilder declared:

> As [civilization] approached, the wild animals of the forest (like the aboriginals) receded, and to enjoy the society of the latter, in preference to that of his fellow-country men, Colonel Boone found himself necessitated to follow their example.[62]

Wilder characterized Boone as living entirely by hunting, and Cole readily accepted that view. Cole's vignette of the dead and bloody deer at Boone's feet and the presence of his hungry dog reinforces this notion of a primitive, half-savage man retreating from civilization and living in the bosom of nature.

Wilder's book also included Lord Byron's eulogy to Boone from *Don Juan*. Its text relates to another aspect of Cole's conception of Boone, as it appears that the artist struggled to reconcile several conflicting ideas about Boone that are also present in Wilder's text.[63] Byron's poem contains the lines:

> The Colonel Boone, backwoodsman of Kentucky
> Was happiest amongst mortals any where;
> For killing nothing but a bear or buck, he
> Enjoyed the lonely, vigorous, harmless days
> Of his old age, in wilds of deepest maze.
> Crime came not near him—she is not the child
> Of solitude; health shrank not from him—for
> Her home is the rarely trodden wild, …
> … Boone lived hunting up to ninety …[64]

In keeping with Byron's poem, in which Boone was described as "An active hermit, even in age the child of

22

nature ..." (stanza 62), in Cole's contradictory depiction of the pioneer, Boone is represented not as a confident hero, but as a withdrawn, hermit-like recluse. He is enshrined beneath trees that are joined just above his head in a form that suggests the arch of a Gothic cathedral. Thus to the image of Boone as a white-Indian, an aged, irascible-looking figure in buckskins and purple leggings, Cole adds yet another layer of meaning—that of a hermit reposing in front of his decrepit log cabin.

Cole placed Boone in the midst of an inaccessible wilderness where tangled growth threatens to surround him and swallow the cabin. This image was present in Wilder's text: "At the age of 65 [Boone] removed ... to the Tennessee Country, then almost a perfect Wilderness, where he built him a log cabin, and for several years enjoyed undisturbed repose," and where "he had for a very considerable time the exclusive and uninterrupted hunting of and destroying [of wild animals] at his pleasure."[65] Boone's wilderness setting is filled with stern sublimity, particularly in the brilliant light that falls on the distant shore of Great Osage Lake. But on closer inspection, it, like its possessor, is hardly an inviting depiction of a Western landscape that would be attractive to settlers looking for fertile flat bottom lands for cultivation. Furthermore, Boone's isolation is absolute, for there is no sign of any other human habitation, not even the plume of smoke rising in the distance.

Cole has envisioned his landscape to suggest a pristine wilderness. The artist often depicted American scenery in a manner calculated to appeal to the growing nostalgia of his well-to-do patrons for an earlier time when the frontier was still unthreatened by the ambitions of lower-class men like Boone who would transform the landscape for utilitarian purposes. To emphasize this visually, Cole utilizes every expressive device at his disposal. The impenetrable vegetation surrounding him forbids access to his dwelling, creating a natural barrier to intrusion. At right, further reinforcing the idea of solitude, Cole relies on a Romantic tradition of symbolism that endowed nature with vitalistic powers. By contriving a large rock at the right to resemble a huge human head in profile, Cole creates an emblematic presence that gazes out protectively toward Boone and the distant landscape over which he is the solitary guardian.[66]

Cole's painting is a complex statement embodying a conservative ideological vision of the West. It emphatically rejects the idea of Boone as a heroic figure opening frontier lands to settlement—the providentially-ordained figure Filson had promoted who leads a chosen people to claim the wilderness. Because of his own orientation and his reliance on Wilder's text, Cole's picture could only appeal to a limited group of wealthy Easterners, and it never attained popular acceptance as a defining image. Cole's painting is the antithesis of both William Ranney's and George C. Bingham's depictions of Boone painted nearly a quarter of a century later. The later works are expansive and optimistic, which Cole and his patrons would have found abhorrent.

Figure 15. Enrico Causici, *The Conflict Between Daniel Boone and the Indians*. 1826-27. Marble relief. United States Capitol, Washington, D.C. Photograph: Office of the Architect of the Capitol.

CHAPTER IV

Defining a Frontier Hero in Jacksonian America:
Boone in the 1830s

Following the election of Andrew Jackson in 1828, the literary image of Daniel Boone that Filson had fabricated and that Cole and Bryan had embellished began to fragment along sectional and party lines. Westerners constituted by far the largest market for Boone literature and images. With their emerging power and wealth they preferred "authentic" images of Boone as a hero, not dissimilar to the type Filson had created. This was the exemplary frontiersman, brave Indian fighter, and man of the people, later so strongly associated with the liberal, even radical democrats of Andrew Jackson's party.

The appetite in the West for a realistic, less idealized image of Boone as a lower-class man of action is understandable when viewed in an economic and social context. The West was the place for ambitious, self-made men on the make: land speculators, settlers hoping to improve their lot, fast buck "Boosters" or confidence men who hoped to exploit the land and the law for a quick profit.

As settlers moved farther west the enormous potential of the land for future development was abundantly evident. However, the greatest remaining impediment to fulfilling hopes for easy wealth through westward expansion were the Native Americans. Settlers fiercely coveted the ancestral territories of American Indians. Western interests eager to expand the American empire and increase their own wealth demanded the removal, or better, the elimination, of the Native Americans.[67]

In response to these pressures numerous revisions and elaborations of Filson's narrative appeared. One of the earliest was by James Hall. His depiction of Boone as brave and adventurous hunter appeared in his *Letters from the West* from 1822-1828. In his *Letters* Hall attempted to reassure his Eastern audience that the noble frontiersman would not regress into a white-Indian in the backwoods of America, even though simultaneously Hall attempted to please his Western readers by representing his Boone as a man who turns his back on civilization, rejoicing in the adventurous life of the hunter.

Another Western version of Boone appeared in John A.

McClung's *Sketches of Western Adventure*. It was published in 1832 and went through nine editions. McClung, as a true Westerner, had no patience with Filson's literary flourishes or Hall's indecisive conception of the Kentuckian. McClung's Boone was a man of daring action, a solitary hunter who would rather fight Indians than rhapsodize about the beauties of a sylvan wilderness landscape as Filson's Boone had done. Like Timothy Flint's account of the following year, it was a runaway best seller.

Timothy Flint, another Western writer, attempted a more moderate and balanced portrayal of Boone. His popular narrative would have considerable influence on Horatio Greenough and William Ranney's depiction of Boone's encounters with the Indians. Flint was intent on explaining the West as a symbolic confrontation between civilization and savagery, and the inevitable replacement of the latter by the former. Flint's Boone is an obliging servant of civilization, not of nature or the hunt. He is proud of his role as a pathfinder for the more developed social order that will follow him. He manifests a sense of self-restraint, even in his relationships with the Indians, that was calculated to appeal to Eastern readers.

These conflicting aspects of Daniel Boone—violent Indian fighter or willing servant of civilization—were vividly symbolized in two sculptures commissioned for the U. S. Capitol. These works were created during the period when the Jacksonian Democrats with their commitment to Western interests began to take power, and their execution coincided with heated debates in congress about controversial proposals to remove Indians from their ancestral lands.

In order to provide official iconic justification in the Capitol Rotunda for the aggressive expansion of the nation into Indian territories, the government turned to the Italian trained sculptor Enrico Causici to create a relief entitled *The Conflict Between Daniel Boone and the Indians* **(Figure 15)**.[68] It was one of a series of four panels intended to depict encounters of settlers with Native Americans.

Although Causici's sculpture was almost exactly contemporaneous with Cole's painting it would be difficult

Figure 16.
Horatio Greenough, *The Rescue*. 1836-53. Marble, h: 11'9"; w: 10'2". United States Capitol, Washington, D.C. Photograph: Office of the Architect of the Capitol.

Figure 17.
Artist Unknown, *Daniel Boone Protects his Family*. 1874. Lithograph, 33" x 38". Collection A.G. Edwards and Sons, Inc., St. Louis.

to imagine two more contrasting representations of Boone. Where Cole had represented a hermit in solitary communion with nature, Causici depicted Boone vanquishing an Indian in brutal hand-to-hand combat, with another lying dead at his feet. Boone's cultural superiority is evident in the prominent position of his Kentucky long rifle that bisects the composition, a symbol of white technology that divides the struggling figures. While the face of the Indian is contorted in cruelty, Boone's face possesses a noble profile that expressed the sentiments of a nation confident of its inevitable triumph over the forces of savagery. Given the official nature of the commission, Dawn Glanz observes, "it is reasonable to assume that Boone was here meant to represent American (i.e. Anglo-Saxon) civilization, superior to and victorious over the Indian savages."[69]

The conflict between civilization and savagery was also the theme of another official commission for a platform in front of the Capitol: Horatio Greenough's monumental, free-standing sculpture *The Rescue* (Figure 16).[70] It was begun in 1836 and finished in 1853. Although Greenough never specifically acknowledged that the work was intended to be directly associated with Daniel Boone, its currency as a tacit symbol of the heroic pioneer was made explicit in a popular lithograph published in 1874, which transposed the figures in Greenough's sculpture into the image of *Daniel Boone Protects his Family* (Figure 17).

The literary source of Greenough's heroic rescuer was almost certainly Timothy Flint's *Biographical Memoir of Daniel Boone*, first published in 1833 and reprinted numerous times over the next two decades. In Flint's narrative the captivity of Boone's and Callaway's daughters is considerably elaborated upon from Filson's abbreviated account, and one part of Flint's text was entitled "They pursue the Indians and rescue the captives." In his narrative, Flint provided a specific verbal image that Greenough adapted for the unusual spatial relationship found in his sculpture that positions Boone subduing the Indian by standing behind him. No other contemporary account of Boone's actions was as precise in its description of this incident. Immediately prior to this key passage Flint informed his readers that the Indians were armed with tomahawks. Flint described "the rescue" this way:

> The grand object now was to get possession of the prisoners without arousing their captors . . . . Boone crawled around, so as to reach the waking Indian from behind, intending to spring upon him and strangle him . . . . But, unfortunately, this Indian instead of being asleep was wide awake . . . . The shadow of Boone coming on them from behind, aroused him. He sprang erect, and uttered a yell . . . .[71]

Greenough introduces a tomahawk into the Indian's hand and transforms Boone's abducted daughters into the figure of a mother and child. But the curious restraint of Greenough's towering figure of the pioneer pinioning the Indian from behind is consistent with the moderate, civilized figure of Boone that Flint's account presented.

As a Federalist and a conservative, Greenough made plain the larger intentions of his group in a letter in which he stated that he endeavored ". . . to convey the idea of the triumph of the whites over the savage tribes, at the same time as it illustrates the dangers of peopling the country."[72] Evidently the artist's intentions were readily understood. Edward G. Loring, a friend of Greenough's, described the finished work in 1859:

> The mother and child were before the Indian and she, in maternal instinct was shielding her child from his grasp, to prevent which the husband seized both arms of the Indian, and bears him down at the same time; so the group told its story of the peril of the American wilderness, the ferocity of the Indians, the superiority of the white man, and how and why civilization crowded the Indian from his soil, with the episode of the woman and infant and the sentiments which belong to them.[73]

It is clear that Greenough was well aware of Causici's relief in the rotunda, and that he felt competition with the earlier work, because in a letter of July 1, 1837 he asserted that he would make a group to "commemorate the dangers and difficulty of peopling our continent, and which shall also serve as a memorial to the Indian race . . . a subject which . . . has not been exhausted by the gentleman whose bas reliefs adorn the Rotunda . . . ."[74]

Greenough's sculpture was particularly significant because as a symbolic variation on the Boone type it was the first visual image of the pioneer to include a woman and child, thereby expanding the definition of Boone's mission in the wilderness to include the family, a motif that Flint had also emphasized. Until Greenough's work, the definition of Boone or the pioneers' calling had remained adamantly gender specific. The sculptor enlarged the theme to embrace women and children. These were added as they had been in Flint's account, to serve as easily comprehended symbols of innocence, virtue, and refinement. In this official state icon that greeted visitors entering the Capitol, Greenough dispelled the notion that frontiersmen living in the wilderness might be tempted to adopt Indian ways and revert to the dreaded white-Indian because with women present men could better resist the primitive lure of Indian ways.

Ironically, given the symbolic importance of the mother and child, the proportions of Greenough's figures are strangely distorted. "The woman is exceptionally diminutive when compared with the Indian, while the rescuer is so giantesque as to make the Indian seem adolescent," Slotkin notes. "Yet the giant's whole purpose is centered on the small woman and tiny infant; it is for them that he exerts his strength."[75] In Jacksonian America, a woman—even a small, out-of-scale one—could still represent the values of civilization threatened by savagery.

The typological symbolism of Greenough's group was unambiguous to mid-century Americans. An anonymous writer in the *Bulletin of the American Art-Union* summarized its racial, nationalistic and progressive meaning.

The thought embodied in the action of the group, and immediately communicated to every spectator is the natural and necessary superiority of the Anglo-Saxon to the Indian. It typifies the settlement of the American continent, and the respective destinies of the two races who here come into collision. You see the exposure and suffering of the female emigrant—the ferocious and destructive instinct of the savage, and his easy subjugation under the superior manhood of the new colonist.

He [the pioneer] whose destiny is to convert forests into cities; who conquers only to liberate, enlighten and elevate . . . he is the type of your own glorious nation . . . .[76]

There were a number of other, less well-known images of Boone created during the mid-1830s. The most important of these were John Gadsby Chapman's portrait of a seated Boone, and William Allan's "official" portrait of Boone that was acquired by the Kentucky legislature for the Capitol in lieu of Chester Harding's life portrait.

Chapman's picture, published in the Cincinnati *Family Magazine* of March 1836 **(Figure 18)**, was a full-length figure engraved on wood by William Redfield.[77] It depicts a handsome and placid Boone attired in buckskins trimmed with a fur collar and a wide felt hat. He is posed casually on a rock overlooking a commanding view of a distant, but indistinct, landscape. Chapman's image is evidently a variation of the Harding/Lewis engraving combined with the James B. Longacre reinterpretation of Harding's full-length portrait that had been published the previous year in Longacre's *National Portrait Gallery of Distinguished Americans* **(Figure 9)**. It is not known whether Chapman's image was based on a lost painting. The mood of the image closely corresponds to the portrayal of Boone as a common man that Timothy Flint had presented in his 1833 book.

Alonzo Chappell's portrait of Boone was created for a later edition of James Longacre's *National Portrait Gallery of Distinguished Americans* published in 1861 **(Figure 19)**. It is basically a variant on the original Harding portrait of Boone with the addition of the meditative sentiments that appear in John G. Chapman's picture. Chappell clearly drew upon the Harding image of Boone in a fur-collar coat while the head of the figure is derived from Longacres' 1835 print. The emphasis in Chappell's image is now firmly on Boone as a distinguished American, but still a man of the people with his hand-sewn buckskin jacket, fur cap, faithful long rifle,

Figure 18. After John Gadsby Chapman, *Daniel Boone*. In the *Family Magazine* (Cincinnati) Vol.1, No. 3 (March 1836), page 81. Oberlin College Library.

and dog. He is situated in a wilderness landscape. The combination of a thoughtful, meditative Boone placed in a prairie-like wilderness was an image of the pioneer that conformed with the "authentic" Daniel Boone, man of the people, that appeared in Peck and Flint's biographies. It was the perfect personification of the philosopher-democrat that antebellum America admired.

In 1840 the Kentucky Legislature appropriated $250 for the purchase of William Allan's (active c. 1834-1848) life-sized representation of Boone **(Figure 20)**.[78] Allan's picture was painted 16 years after Boone's death and was fanciful in both characterization and setting.[79] Allan's picture did, however, contain all the elements required for a portrait of Boone in the late 1830s and early 1840s. It presented him as the archetype of the hunter and backwoodsman, and its reliance on Harding's and Chapman's images are apparent in its fur collar coat and the relaxed seated pose of the pioneer. Like Chapman's figure, Boone is seated in a frontal position, his facial profile and prominent brow exaggerated to symbolize powers of genius commonly promoted in phrenological theories of the period.

Figure 19. After a lost painting by Alonzo Chappell, *Daniel Boone*, from James B. Longacre, *National Portrait Gallery of Distinguished Americans*, The St. Louis Mercantile Library Association.

Figure 20. William C. Allan, *Daniel Boone*. 1839. Oil on canvas, 103 x 64 1/2". Kentucky History Museum Collection, Kentucky Historical Society, Frankfort, Kentucky.

Allan, like Chapman and Harding, clad his pathfinder in fringed buckskins and beaded Indian moccasins, alluding, as was the custom by the late 1830s, to Boone's adapting of Indian customs. His reddish-brown coat creates a dramatic effect. Characteristically, Allan's Boone holds a Kentucky long rifle, almost as if he were presenting it for the viewer to inspect. In the foreground at his feet is his dog. Surrounding him is a dark and tangled forest interior with gnarled trees and rocks, while at the left a path leads from the seated pioneer out to a distant, brightly lit clearing.

The depictions of Boone created during the Jacksonian period presented the visual image of the pioneer in transition from the hermitism of Cole's painting toward a personification of Boone as a national figure—an heroic Western man of the people who would become the dominant symbol of the pioneer in the paintings of William Ranney and George Caleb Bingham in the late 1840s and early 1850s.

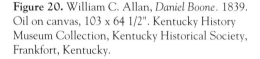

Figure 21. William T. Ranney, *Daniel Boone's First View of Kentucky.* 1849.
Oil on canvas, 36" x 53 1/2". The Thomas Gilcrease Institute of American History and Art, Tulsa, Oklahoma.

CHAPTER V

The Columbus of the Woods:
William Ranney's Daniel Boone as the Type of a National Hero

By the late 1840s images of heroic Western types were being elevated to the status of national symbols to represent the spirit of exploration, conquest, and enterprise as artists and writers sought symbols of national identity. Daniel Boone came to symbolize during that decade the most important empire builder of early American history. Boone was again reconstructed in literature and painting to serve as a prime symbol of the common man's contributions to building a democracy. William Ranney and George Caleb Bingham would represent this idea in their paintings of Boone—an heroic figure who, despite his common origins, manifested the energy of divine intercession in the triumphant national march to the West. It was no coincidence that the symbolism of Daniel Boone as the type of a national hero reached its zenith of popularity in the visual arts during the period of expansion following the Mexican War and the California Gold Rush when the future scope of the nation seemed virtually unlimited.

Beginning in the late 1830s a revival of interest resulted in images calculated to underscore the heroic aspects of early American history.[80] Paintings of Western types such as fur trappers, mountain men, and Western riverboat men by Charles Deas, William Ranney, and George Caleb Bingham first became popular during this period.[81] Their pictures visually legitimized the recent conquests of new territory in the West.[82] Indeed, Thomas Cole, who had earlier been so disapproving of the westward movement, proposed around 1845 to profit from the opportunity by painting "Daniel Boone looking from the eminence over the vast forest and seeing the Ohio for the first time———," although he never undertook the work.[83]

William Ranney's two versions of *Daniel Boone's First View of Kentucky*, **(Color Plate 3, Figures 21, 24),** were major expressions of the national cultural discourse that underlay the first great outpouring of Western images during the late 1840s.[84] Ranney's picture of Boone perfectly represented the fantasy of an effortless claiming of the West by a band of pioneers. The theatrical gestures of Ranney's motionless figures of genrefied history were influenced by

passages in the *Biographical Memoir of Daniel Boone* by Timothy Flint, which remained enormously popular through numerous reprinted and pirated editions. Ranney merged verbal images from Flint's narrative with John Mason Peck's more recently published *Life of Daniel Boone, the Pioneer of Kentucky* that appeared in 1847, just before the artist began his work. Both books claimed to have been based on personal interviews with the Kentuckian, and both presented a new image of Boone as a man of the common people.

The composition of Ranney's painting was strongly influenced by a simple woodcut, perhaps by William Woodruff, published in Flint's book **(Figure 23)**. A drawing in pencil on pink paper shows an intermediate conception of the image as Ranney modified the woodcut image **(Figure 24)**. Ranney's picture was immediately acquired by the American Art-Union, which raffled it, and issued a print of the work in their *Bulletin* **(Figure 22)**. Ranney, like other artists, eagerly sought the patronage of the Art-Union because of the national visibility it provided.

The reliance on an image from Flint's book and on specific passages in Flint's biography of Boone is especially significant in decoding Ranney's representation of the Western pioneer. Flint was a journalist working in Cincinnati and his account was particularly notable because it was the first to go beyond a mere recycling of Filson's original narrative. Flint had met Boone briefly in 1816, and later interviewed Boone's surviving family. He carefully researched newspaper reports and gathered anecdotes into a substantially new and much enlarged account of the hero. Flint subdued the image of Boone as the free and easy hunter of the frontier, but carefully retained the idea that Boone was "endowed by Providence for the part which he was called upon to act." According to Flint, Boone "... received his commission for his achievements ... from the sign manual of nature."[85] Throughout the book Flint presents Boone as the quintessential backwoodsman and hunter, concluding with the apostrophe: "In all future time, and in every portion of the globe, in history, in sculpture, in song, in eloquence— the name of Daniel Boone will be recorded as the patriarch

Figure 22. Engraved by Alfred Jones after William Ranney's *Daniel Boone's First View of Kentucky*, engraving on paper, 5 1/2" x 8". In the *Bulletin of the American Art-Union*, May 1850, (No.195). Library Company, Philadelphia.

Figure 23. Woodcut by William Woodruff published in Timothy Flint, *The Life and Exploits of Col. Daniel Boone.* (Cincinnati: Morgan, 1850). Stratford Lee Morton Collection, Special Collections, Olin Library, Washington University, St. Louis.

of backwoods Pioneers."[86] Flint's Boone "worshipped, as he often said, the Great Spirit—for the woods were his books and his temple...."[87] In Flint's presentation Boone was a representative of all that was best in the Western character, and hence all that would be valuable to the nation expanding across the continent. It was a literary image that would be especially useful to a New York artist painting for the American Art-Union in the late 1840s.

Flint's book was important for Ranney, but the single most significant text influencing painted images of Daniel Boone in the late 1840s and early 1850s was John Mason Peck's *Life of Daniel Boone, the Pioneer of Kentucky*. It was published in 1847 in Jared Sparks' multi-volume *Library of American Biography*. Peck was a Westerner and a minister who was intent on assuaging Eastern fears of the West by representing Boone as a trustworthy citizen. His Boone was a pioneer who upheld the best traditions of Christian values. Peck was the first writer to draw upon the work of Lyman Draper of Baltimore, who had already begun to amass an enormous archive of material about Boone. Because of Peck's efforts to be more "objective," his account eliminated the heroicized aspects of earlier versions of Boone's life and resulted in a more "authentic" if less dramatic depiction.

Peck begins his book by disputing the conventional image of Boone as a fierce Indian fighter that official art had depicted.

> *In the rotunda of the Capitol . . . are sculptured emblems of incidents in the early history of our country. The one [by Enrico Causici, **Figure 15**] . . . represents a brawny white man in deadly conflict with two Indians. One lies at his feet in the agonies of death; the other, with uplifted tomahawk, is about to give the fatal stroke, when he is paralyzed by the hunter's knife. This was intended to represent an incident in the life of Boone, but unfortunately, it is wholly fictious.*[88]

Peck's purpose was to depict Boone as the typical common man—the reliable pioneer type who is the mainstay of a democratic nation of middle-class settlers. He unhesitatingly criticizes Flint's book as being "too much colored by the visions of the writer's affluent imagination."[89]

Peck took pains to dispel the idea that Boone was aggressive or unfeeling in his manners. "Daniel Boone, far from possessing a ferocious temper, or exhibiting dissatisfaction with the charms of domestic and social life, was mild, humane, and charitable; his manners were gentle, his address conciliating, and his heart open to friendship and hospitality."[90] In visually articulating these attributes of Boone's personality Ranney's depiction of the pioneer as a gentle and approachable man of the people is clearly influenced primarily by Peck.

The earlier image of Boone as a wild-eyed frontiersman who rejected civilization is emphatically repudiated in Ranney's picture, and by Peck, who declared:

> *The various tales told of the prejudices of Colonel Boone against civilization and social enjoyments are fictitious. He was not anti-social in his feeling and sympathies. He loved his fellow creatures; he loved his children; he sympathized with suffering and oppressed humanity....*[91]

Ranney, like Peck, seems especially interested in Boone's class. Peck adds a new note of middle-class justification for Boone's decision to move west because of disgust with the "extravagant modes of living" in North Carolina, the injustice of "Labor, among the opulent ... performed by slaves, [while] the industrious white man, who kept no servants, but ... worked the farm, was less respected than his more opulent neighbors...." "Under these circumstances," Peck states, "men of quiet habits, opposed to luxury and oppression, migrated to the wilderness beyond the mountains, where they could enjoy independence and a share of respectability."[92]

Throughout his carefully researched narrative Peck does not represent Boone as an instrument of American expansion, and his book is unusual for its time because it avoids the shrill rhetoric of Manifest Destiny. In the conclusion, however, Peck succumbs, as does Ranney, to the idea of Boone as a symbol of divine intervention by appending to his text Governor Morehead's 1840 addressed commemorating the first settlement of Kentucky. Morehead went right to the point by recalling Filson's evocation of Boone as "an instrument *ordained* to settle the wilderness." Although in general harmony with Peck's objective of representing Boone as the personification of the quintessential "common man," Morehead declared in Boone's defense that "[Boone] came, therefore, not to establish the foundations of a great state, nor to extend the empire of civilization, but because it *was* a wilderness...."[93] "Where Peck's account of Boone seeks to make Boone respectable in conventional Eastern terms," Slotkin notes, "Morehead's eulogy places Boone in his proper rung of society, above the rung of his class but inferior to the true leaders of American society."[94]

The texts that Ranney relied upon provide an insight into the formulation of his pictures, and the fundamental concept of national control over the West by the common man. Flint's account might have also suggested an idea for the landscape setting of Ranney's picture. Although the passage is lengthy it is a valuable gloss on Ranney's representation of the scene.

> *The last crags and cliffs of the middle ridges having been scrambled over, on the following morning they stood on the summit of the Cumberland Mountain, the farthest western spur of this line of heights. From this point the descent into the great western valley began. What a scene opened before them! A feeling of the sublime is inspired in every bosom susceptible of it, by a view from any point of these vast ranges, of the boundless forest valleys of the*

Figure 24. William T. Ranney, *Daniel Boone's First View of Kentucky*. 1849.
Oil on canvas, 36" x 53 1/2". Anschutz Collection, Denver.

Figure 25. Study for William T. Ranney, *Daniel Boone's First View of Kentucky*. 1769. Pencil on pink paper, 9" x 12". J.B. Speed Art Museum, Louisville, Kentucky.

Ohio. It is a view more grand, more heart stirring than that of the ocean. Illimitable extents of woods, and winding river courses spread before them like a large map. "Glorious country!" they exclaimed. Little did Boone dream that in fifty years, immense portions of it would pass from the domain of the hunter [i.e. the Indians], and its waters be navigated by nearly two hundred steamboats, sweeping down these streams that now rolled through the unbroken forests before them. To them it stood forth an unexplored paradise of the hunter's imagination.

After a long pause, in thoughts too deep for words, they began the descent . . . .

From an eminence . . . they could see, as far as vision could extend, the beautiful country of Kentucky. They remarked with astonishment the tall, straight trees, shading the exuberant soil, wholly clear from any other underbrush than the rich cane-brakes, the image of verdure and luxuriance, or a tall grass and clover. Down the gentle slopes murmured clear limestone brook. Finley [sic] who had some touch of scripture knowledge exclaimed in view of

this wilderness-paradise . . . "This wilderness blossoms as the rose; these desolate places are as the garden of God."[95]

For Ranney as for Flint, and before him Filson, the ascent to the summit, or the "commanding ridge" as it was so aptly described in Filson's original text, is a critical moment in the pathfinder's opening of the West. From the summit "visual conquest," the assertion of an ocular claim of proprietorship on behalf of the nation is made effortlessly, endorsed by biblical associations of prosperity in a "wilderness-paradise."

In Ranney's painting six white men gaze from a pulpit-like platform high over the distant landscape—a "paradise of the imagination," where "they could see as far as vision could extend..." a scene in which "millions of freemen" will displace Indians and the rivers are to be tamed by "nearly two hundred steamboats." Biblical verses are enjoined by Flint to make the transformation of this wilderness appear to be the result of historical inevitability, subtly invoking the well-used typological artifices common to the rhetoric of

Manifest Destiny. Ranney's picture substantiates the belief that American pioneers merely by the act of visually claiming the land were fulfilling God's promise, and for them the wilderness would "blossom as the rose."

Ranney's image relied on a convention of landscape perception that was well understood in his period. For 19th-century Americans the ascent of a promontory could provide the tourist, or even vicariously the spectator of a painting, with "a sudden access of power, a dizzying sense of having suddenly come into possession of terrain stretching as far as the eye could see," as Alan Wallach has demonstrated in a recent article.[96] Wallach's discussion of the "panoptic sublime" in Cole's painting *The Oxbow* exposes the importance of the "sovereign gaze" or "eye of power" as he terms it. Drawing upon the ideas of Michel Foucault, Wallach discusses how the relationship between the artist's exercise of vision and the operation of ideology and power functioned in one of Cole's most important paintings. It is a relationship in which the spectator of Ranney's picture is also invited to participate, not so much through the experience of a vast panorama of space as in Cole's *Oxbow*, but through the dreamy gazes of Boone's party contemplating their own glorious future as well as the nation's, in the conquest of the landscape "as far as vision will extend."

The specific manner in which Boone was to be represented as a symbol of the common man of the West was a problem for Ranney that was solved by a close reading of Peck's *Life of Daniel Boone*. In that text the pathfinder's clothes were precisely described.

> ... *Their dress was of the description usually worn at that period by all forest rangers. The outside garment was a hunting shirt, or loose, open frock, made of dressed deer skins. Leggins or drawers, of the same material, covered the lower extremities, to which was appended a pair of moccasins for the feet. The cape or collar of the hunting shirt, and the seams of the leggins were adorned with fringes. The undergarments were of coarse cotton. A leathern belt encircled the body; on the right side was suspended the tomahawk, to be used as a hatchet; on the left side was the hunting-knife, powder-horn, bullet-pouch, and other appendages indispensable for a hunter... ."*[97]

It is particularly interesting to note in Peck's description the reference to Boone carrying a tomahawk, "to be used as a hatchet." This weapon is omitted by Ranney from both versions of his picture. An allusion to a "tomahawk" skirted dangerously close to the troublesome issue of Boone's alleged reversion to Indian customs and the imputation that Boone might have taken scalps with his tomahawk. That idea would have been discordant with the expectations of Ranney's audience at the Art-Union.

It is enlightening to compare the drawing **(Figure 25)** for Ranney's picture with the paintings based on it, and it is even more instructive to compare the first and second versions of the painting **(Color Plate 3, Figure 21)** with each other **(Figure 24)**. At first glance these images may appear to be virtually identical, but subtle revisions occur in the representation of Boone and his company. These changes are directly related to differences in Flint's conception of Boone as a self-made man who realizes his identity through adaptation to Indian customs, and Peck's portrayal of Boone as a more traditional figure—a protector and conservator of American values. Peck found Boone to be a representative of the "better class" of Western pioneers, but not of the "best class."[98]

In the drawing **(Figure 25)** the approximate positions of the figures in the paintings are established. But the larger issue of the class of pioneers represented by Boone and his company was still in the process of being defined by Ranney. There is a noticeable shift in the characterization of facial expressions from drawing to the paintings. The face of Boone, the bare-headed figure third from the left, is less refined than he appears in the first painted version of the image **(Color Plate 3, Figure 21)**, and considerably less genteel than in the second version **(Figure 24)**. Similarly, the other faces in the party, particularly the figure at the far right, seem wilder and more unkempt in appearance than in the paintings. In effect, Ranney, like Bingham two years later, has taken pains to refine his backwoodsmen. In the drawing Boone and his band are members of a rough, slovenly lower-class. In the paintings they are represented as well-bred Americans. In the drawing Boone's party is probably depicted more like the actual rough-and-ready frontiersmen that Ranney had met and sketched on this 1836 trip west to enlist in the Texas Army during the War with Mexico—the lowest class of men. In the first painted version they are a "better class" of pioneer, but in the second, final painted version they have become representatives of the "best class."

In the first version of the painting, as in the drawing, there is evidence that Ranney was fascinated with the idea of Boone's primitivism **(Color Plate 3, Figure 21)**. A close reading of some key details of Boone's costume suggests a clear admiration for Indian customs as they had been adapted by the trappers and mountain men Ranney had met during his travels in the West. In the first version, Boone is represented with a considerable number of Indian accoutrements, such as his red moccasins and beaded and heavily fringed buckskin coat. In the later version **(Figure 24)** the moccasins are replaced by ordinary leather boots, and his fringed jacket and colorful trade blanket is replaced by more conventional gear.

In the earlier image, Boone displays a heavy growth of beard, but in the later version he is virtually clean shaven. Similarly, Findley, the figure to the left of Boone in the earlier Art-Union picture, is shown in buckskins and moccasins, in the second version he is in a green cloth coat and wearing leather shoes. Boone's Kentucky long rifle is

Figure 26. Frontispiece for George Canning Hill, *Daniel Boone, the Pioneer of Kentucky*, (Philadelphia: J.B. Lippincott & Company, 1859). Charles W. Bryan, Jr. Collection, Special Collections, Olin Library, Washington University, St. Louis.

particularly detailed, its flint-lock mechanism clearly visible in both versions. Its position between his legs suggests masculine power, a significant shift from the drawing where he merely leans on the gun.

Through the repeated lines of the guns and the gestures of arms holding them, Ranney creates a compositional momentum from right to left—the source of a warmly beckoning morning light. Interestingly, here again, the first and second versions of the picture offer subtle but telling differences. In the first version of the painting the landscape is rougher and less inviting, but in the second the sky is warmer, while the background is appealing with more trees and a less precipitous drop to the valley below.

There are also subtle shifts in the arrangements of the figures and their expressions. In the second version Boone is highlighted more effectively. He is placed at the exact center of the composition, and the surrounding figures are separated so that he is more emphatically outlined. In the second

version, the figure at right leaning on his gun just behind the dogs wears an expression of dreamy anticipation at the prospect of taking his share of the landscape they survey. Even the pair of dogs seem caught up in the fantasy, their wide-eyed gaze underscoring the bountiful prospects of game for man and animal alike.

With one major exception, contemporary reviews of Ranney's painting were sparse. *The Literary World* noted that, "Ranney is living at Weehawken. He has had in hand for several months past a composition called, 'The Encampment of Boone,' taken from the life of that distinguished pioneer."[99]

It was not until 1852 that Henry T. Tuckerman commented extensively on Ranney's painting in an article titled "Over the Mountains." It was a long account of the heroic deeds of Daniel Boone published in *The Home Book of the Picturesque*. Tuckerman's article was largely a conflation of ideas and images from Flint and Peck with notions of Boone's philosophizing derived from Lord Byron's poem. The generative impulse behind the lengthy commentary was Tuckerman's admiration for Ranney's painting. Tuckerman's interpretation provides an insight into how Ranney's picture was read in the early 1850s. The passage compels elucidation with its implicit assumptions about Boone and his place in the course of national history. The idea that the Alleghenies have a "moral interest" because of their associations with the pathfinder who went "over the mountains" to "found a State in the wilderness" would be echoed nearly four decades later in the verbal imagery of Tuckerman's frontier thesis.

> *There hung for many months, on the walls of the Art-Union gallery in New York, a picture by Ranney, so thoroughly national in its subject and true to nature in its execution, that it was refreshing to contemplate it . . . . It represented a flat ledge of rock, the summit of a high cliff that projected over a rich, umbrageous country, upon which a band of hunters leaning on their rifles, were gazing with looks of delighted surprise. The foremost . . . is pointing out the landscape to his comrades, with an air of exultant yet calm satisfaction . . . . his loose hunting shirt, his easy attitude, the fresh brown tint of his cheek, and an ingenuous, cheerful, determined yet benign expression of countenance, proclaim the hunter and pioneer, the Columbus of the woods, the forest philosopher and brave champion. The picture represents Daniel Boone discovering to his companions the fertile levels of Kentucky.*[100]

Tuckerman observed that Ranney's work was "thoroughly national in its subject and true to nature in its execution" so that it was "refreshing to contemplate it, after being wearied with far more ambitious yet less successful attempts." This almost surely is an allusion to Bingham's painting of Boone which was rejected by the American Art-Union in the spring of 1851, just as Tuckerman was completing his essay.

Undoubtedly, the most intriguing comment is Tuckerman's reference to Boone as "the Columbus of the woods," from which this exhibition derives part of its title. The phrase resonates with the concepts of typology, implying that Boone is a successor to Columbus, and therefore a figure who stands in a direct line leading back to the Italian explorer. The typological notion of a genealogy of explorers and pioneers was made explicit a few years later in the frontispiece of George Canning Hills' book *Daniel Boone, the Pioneer of Kentucky* published in 1859 **(Figure 26)**. In that image a figure representing an American Indian holds up a medallion with the face of the pathfinder. Beside her sits a Caucasian female holding books and a pen. She represents Clio, the muse of history. Behind the medallion of Boone is a tablet with the names "Columbus, Americus [Vespucci], Cabot, Raleigh"—all famous explorers who had preceded Boone in opening the New World.[101] Linking Boone with earlier conquerors conferred legitimacy on the famous Kentuckian who was also, according to Tuckerman, echoing Filson, a "forest philosopher and brave champion." Tuckerman's commentary on Ranney's painting makes explicit the idealistic associations personified in Boone as the common man who was free of "the spirit of trade and political ambitions."

> *Such a man forms an admirable progenitor in that nursery of character—the West; and a fine contrast to the development elsewhere induced by the spirit of trade and political ambitions . . . —his character indicates for the descendants of the hunters and pioneers, a brave, independent and noble ancestry . . . . Thus . . . the western pioneer is an object of peculiar interest; and the career of Boone is alike distinguished for its association with romantic adventure and historical fact.*[102]

Here in a nutshell is the essence of Ranney's Boone. He is the type of a national hero, descendant of "hunters and pioneers." Boone represents the essence of the Western freeman of "a brave, independent and noble [Anglo-Saxon] ancestry." The future of the nation as it expands west—"that nursery of character"—will turn out well if it is entrusted to men like Ranney's Daniel Boone.

Ranney's painting represents an ambitious attempt to visualize Boone as national hero, and to symbolically rehearse the emotions of the nation determined to assert its control over vast Western territories. By 1847 Kentucky and the Ohio Valley had long since been incorporated into the Union, but the landscape beyond the Mississippi beckoned to a new generation of settlers. It was to their aspirations for possession that the cultural discourse about claiming the West embodied in Ranney's picture was ultimately addressed.

In 1852 William Ranney painted a second image of Daniel Boone. His *Squire Boone Crossing the Mountains with Stores for His Brother Daniel, Encamped in the Wilds of Kentucky* was exhibited at the National Academy of Design Annual Exhibition the following year **(Figure 27)**. The subject was an unusual one since it did not directly depict Daniel Boone, but his brother, Squire.[103] Squire Boone's return from North Carolina after the disastrous first attempt to reconnoitre Kentucky in 1770 was included in all major accounts of Boone's life, although Flint's text upon which Ranney relied downplayed Squire's heroism. During Boone's first expedition to Kentucky with his brother and another man, "they were in want of many things. Clothing and moccasins they might supply. With bread, sugar, and salt, they could dispense. But ammunition, an article absolutely indispensable, was failing them."[104] Consequently, Squire left Daniel alone in the wilderness and returned the following spring with supplies.

John M. Peck's *Life of Daniel Boone* was once again useful to the artist, for Peck was very specific in describing Squire Boone's return. "He [Squire] rode one horse, and led another heavily laden with the necessaries required."[105] The critic for *The Home Journal* concisely captured the sentiment of Ranney's painting:

> *This is a spirited and pleasing picture. The gallant backwoodsman is mounted, and is leading a pack horse. He sits in the attitude of one who, knowing himself to be in a dangerous country, has just heard, or fancied he heard, a suspicious noise. The face is an open and bright one; the horses are excellent; the accoutrements and dress of the rider are exceedingly good. We could wish the design of the artist had comprehended a wider expanse of country, or that he had made the scenery a little more distant and characteristic.*[106]

The critic for the *New York Herald* noted: "Boon [sic] is represented on horseback and is evidently listening around if any Indians are near. The bold, careless hunter is well depicted, but perhaps the figure is too youthful."[107] It is instructive to realize that the gesture or gaze of a figure could evoke associations in the mind of critics of hostile Indians lurking just outside the pictorial space. So deeply ingrained were the habits of Indian hating that such thoughts came immediately to mind. These contemporary comments afford important insights into the cultural values implicitly articulated in such an image.

Figure 27. William T. Ranney, *Squire Boone's Crossing the Mountains with Stores for His Brother Daniel, Encamped in the Wilds of Kentucky*. 1852. Oil on canvas, 36" x 32 1/2". Museum of Fine Arts, Springfield, Massachusetts. Gift from the Estate of Amelia Peabody.

Figure 28. George C. Bingham, *Daniel Boone Escorting Settlers Through the Cumberland Gap*. 1851-52.
Oil on canvas, 36 1/2" x 50 1/4". Washington University Gallery of Art, St. Louis. Gift of Nathaniel Phillips, 1890.

CHAPTER VI

An American Moses:
George Caleb Bingham's *Daniel Boone Escorting Settlers Through the Cumberland Gap*

No single work of art has contributed more to establishing Daniel Boone as the quintessential symbol of westward expansion in mid-19th century America than George Caleb Bingham's *The Emigration of Daniel Boone* or *Daniel Boone Escorting Settlers Through the Cumberland Gap* (**Cover, Figure 28**). The picture defined for the period the typology of westward migration—what it had meant for the past, and what it should mean for the present, and especially what it must signify in the *future*. The meaning of this image is as complex as the multitude of thorny social, political, and intellectual issues that faced the young nation in the decade of the 1850s.

Only a few years ago Bingham's paintings seemed to be little more than charming naive American images of a "heroic age," uncluttered by the tensions and politics of the nation at mid-century. Today, however, this view has radically changed, for as Nancy Rash has observed, "His works were embedded in the particular American cultural character of his day—in religion, in partisan political ideas, in a certain view of race and gender."[108] There is incontrovertible evidence of Bingham's absorption in political issues. It first emerges in the early 1840s, the decade leading up to the creation of Bingham's first attempt at painting history in *The Emigration of Daniel Boone*. The painting was created in New York City where Bingham had hopes of selling it to the American Art-Union with its national constituency. Nonetheless, it was in many respects an image conceived with his Western friends and patrons in Missouri in mind. It contained important allusions to Bingham's own political views and even references to the artist's personal history. Furthermore, Bingham was preoccupied with Boone from the 1840s to the 1860s.

The subject was a natural one for the young Missouri artist. Missouri claimed Daniel Boone as one of its own. The area where Boone had settled during his last years was known as "Boonville" or "Boonelick," and Boone County where Bingham resided was also named for him. In his letters Bingham often referred to political and family matters in "Old Boon."

One of Bingham's memories of himself as an aspiring painter growing up on the Missouri frontier in the 1820s was meeting Chester Harding and assisting him in his temporary studio in Franklin, Missouri, when he painted his full-length portrait of Boone. In a letter of 1872, Bingham reminisced, "I was at that time a lad of 10 years old and daily assisted in Harding's studio, and [the] wonder and delight with which his works filled my mind impressed them indelibly upon my then unburthened memory." Bingham continued his recollection of more than half a century earlier by describing the painting of Boone that Harding completed in Frankfort.

> The famous pioneer had spent his last days at a place known as Lieutre Island, on the Missouri river, about sixty miles below Franklin. Harding had visited him in the cabin which sheltered him and made a pencil drawing and perhaps a study in oil from life, but the portrait was completed in his temporary studio in Franklin, and its completion witnessed by myself. Boone died a short time before the portrait was finished.[109]

It is tempting to speculate that the youthful Bingham, whose own father died only three years after the encounter with Harding, may have been stimulated to take up the career of an artist because of his admiration for Harding. The 1872 letter makes clear that the experience of meeting Harding left an indelible impression. Fifty years later Bingham still remembered small details such as the existence of both a pencil drawing and the oil sketch from life that Harding had made of Boone. The subject of Daniel Boone would continue to absorb Bingham's attention for over two decades, leading to one of his most exceptional paintings and also one of the greatest frustrations of his career.

Around 1830, at the age of nineteen, Bingham is said to have painted a signboard for a hotel in Boonesville that depicted "old Daniel Boone in buckskin dress with his gun at his side."[110] It seems likely that Bingham based this advertisement on both his remembrance of Harding's portraits of Boone, and on the print made after it by Harding and James Otto Lewis.

In a large and intricate four-sided political banner

painted in 1840 for the Whigs of Saline County, Missouri, the artist presented a complex visual statement of the Whig party's political agenda. The banner has long since disappeared. But the banner, as well as a partisan speech of 1840, and a famous letter Bingham wrote the following year are powerful evidence of how deeply the artist immersed himself in contemporary politics. The 1841 letter has often been mistakenly interpreted as a declaration of his lack of interest in politics, because it boldly states, "I am a painter and nothing else... ."[111] Nancy Rash recognizes that the context of this letter demonstrates just the opposite: "Bingham embedded [the] statement of his desire to be only a painter in the thickest of political discourse."[112]

The political banner and speech of 1840, and the letter of 1841 demonstrated Bingham's intense absorption in Whig ideology, affirming his commitment to the party and suggesting some of the ways he would work to join art and politics throughout the course of his career. By 1846 he would even sign his letters to his friend and patron James S. Rollins, "Yours in the bonds of Whiggery."[113]

In 1844 the symbolic figure of Daniel Boone dramatically reappears in Bingham's art in a striking proposal for another political banner for the Whigs of Boone County,

Missouri. Unfortunately, these paintings have been lost, probably destroyed by fire in the early 20th century. Bingham was already thinking of creating a permanent work of fine art along with the banner commission, for he added the proviso, "With reference to the banner which you desire for your delegation to our convention, I can merely state that I shall be happy to execute it, provided you allow me to paint it on linnen [sic], the only material on which I can make an effective picture." The large size and explicit Whig political agenda of the banners was also made apparent by the artist: "I am now just beginning one for Cooper, and for Howard [counties], each 7 by 8 feet—on one I shall give a full length portrait of [Henry] Clay as the Statesman with his American System operating in the distance, on the other I shall represent him as the plain farmer of Ashland." Bingham specified the banners "will be so suspended as to be eisily [sic] borne by four men walking in the order of the procession. The cost will be from fifty to sixty dollars each."

The banners were conceived as important works of art by Bingham. "They will be substantial oil pictures and may be preserved as relics of the present political campaign." The centerpiece of the banner's design was to have particular applicability to the Whig cause in Boone County, Missouri, for it would depict:

Figure 29. Claude Regnier (after George C. Bingham), *The Emigration of Daniel Boone*. 1852. Lithograph, 18 5/16" x 23 3/4". The Missouri Historical Society, St. Louis.

. . . *old Daniel Boone himself engaged in one of his death struggles with an Indian, painted as large as life, it would make a picture that would take with the multitude, and also be in accordance with historical truth. It might be emblimatical [sic] also of the early state of the west, while on the other side I might paint a landscape with "peaceful fields and lowing herds" indicative of his present advancement in civilization."*[114]

Bingham's statement is important because it discloses that the artist had already begun to view Boone as a typological personification of American history. This was symbolized by imagery of Boone fighting with Indians, "emblematical of the early state of the west," to the reverse of the banner representing an agrarian landscape symbolic of the "present advancement of civilization." Evidently, Boone's struggle to wrest Western lands from Indians foreshadowed the progress of the nation culminating in a cultivated landscape of "peaceful fields and lowing herds." Because of Boone's popular renown and the widespread understanding of such symbolism Bingham was sure the picture "would take with the multitude."

In 1851, Bingham, who then lived in New York City,

began painting what would be the last and most famous image of Daniel Boone, and the only one of the three still extant. In a long letter to Rollins, filled with scathing comments about the Democrats and the partisans of Senator Thomas Hart Benton, Bingham informed his patron:

I am now painting the emigration of Boone and his family to Kentucky. I do not know whether I will sell it to one of the Art Unions, or have it engraved with the expectation of remunerating myself from the sale of the engraving. The subject is a popular one in the west, and one which has never been painted.[115]

The letter continued with an aside: "...managers of the Art Union display in some cases gross favoritism in the purchase of their pictures," and concluded on a blatantly anti-Semitic note, "and in my transactions with them hereafter, I shall act as if I were dealing with a Jew."

The critic for *The Home Journal* saw the picture in early April, just before Bingham submitted it for purchase at the Art-Union on April 14, 1851. *The Home Journal* critic, in what could have only been considered a back-handed compliment to the artist, noted improvements in Bingham's style:

Figure 30. Thomas Easterly, *George C. Bingham's Daniel Boone Escorting Settlers*. 1854. Daguerreotype, 4 1/4 x 5 1/2". The Missouri Historical Society, St. Louis.

43

Figure 31. George C. Bingham, *Guide*. 1851. Brush, ink, and wash on paper, 12 1/8" x 9 1/8". The Bingham Trust for the People of Missouri. Acquired through the generosity of the Brown Group Inc. Charitable Trust.

—Mr. Bingham is finishing a large work, representing the emigration of Daniel Boone to Kentucky. The composition and the effect here are extremely pleasing, and fully atone for some discrepancies in these points, which we have felt in previous productions of this painter.[116]

The praise was not to suffice, however, and Bingham experienced more than two years of frustration and discouragement in his efforts to sell the picture.

Bingham's first disappointment was to be at the hands of the managers of the American Art-Union, who up to that time had been his most reliable patron. After receiving his picture on April 14, 1851, they declined to purchase the work for their annual distribution. A contract to engrave the work by the prestigious French firm of Goupil & Co. of New York and Paris softened this blow. The painting was shipped to Paris where it was lithographed by Claude Regnier and printed by Lemercier **(Figure 29)**.[117]

This print is a particularly significant object in understanding the development of Bingham's painting and retrieving its hidden meanings. The Goupil lithograph discloses the appearance of the painting in its first state, *before* Bingham extensively reworked the picture, probably around the fall of 1852, according to E. Maurice Bloch.[118] A fascinating daguerreotype photograph of the painting in a final state of completion was made by Thomas Easterly, probably for Bingham's use in attempting to sell the picture **(Figure 30)**.[119] A recent scan of the painting using infrared reflectography revealed that the underpainting in the picture does in fact conform to that seen in the Goupil lithograph.[120] Bingham completed the final state of the picture by late October 1852, because by that date he had exhibited it in Columbia, Missouri, in connection with a raffle. Bloch speculates that the alterations to the picture may reflect Bingham's disappointment with the Goupil lithograph that he had expected would be an engraving. An equally likely

Figure 32. George C. Bingham, *Pioneer* (Flanders Callaway). 1851. Brush, ink, and wash on paper, 14 11/16" x 9 5/8". The Bingham Trust for the People of Missouri. Acquired through the generosity of Emerson Electric Co.

reason for his extensive alterations of the picture might have been the stinging rebuke of his work carried in the December 1851 *Bulletin* of the Art-Union. The writer, whom Bloch has identified as the minor artist Thomas W. Whitley, praised Bingham's Eastern rival William Sidney Mount as "thoroughly succeeding in delineating American life." Bingham, he declared, "has made some good studies of Western character, but so entirely undisciplined and yet mannered, and often mean in subject, and showing such want of earnestness in the repetitions of the same faces, that they are hardly entitled to rank."[121] The artist's reaction to this harsh criticism is unknown, but his dismay may be imagined given his earlier letter to Rollins in which he complained bitterly about the Art-Union's managers.

The differences between the first version of Bingham's painting of Boone and the appearance of the picture as it is known today are useful in understanding how the artist intensified the expression of sentiment in his picture. In repainting the image, Bingham simultaneously strengthened the composition, enriching the effect, while adding important details that subtly altered its meaning. Bingham must have taken seriously the criticism of his picture and its rejection by the Art-Union, for one change was a further idealization of his figures to overcome what had been called their "repetitiousness" and "mean," or common, quality. The extensive reworking of the background was another major change from the earlier image.[122]

While the general arrangement of the four figures in the

Figure 33. Detail. Thomas Cole, *View of Schroon Mountain, Essex Co., New-York, After a Storm.* 1838. Oil on Canvas, 39 3/8" x 63". The Cleveland Museum of Art. The Hinman B. Hurlburt Collection.

Figure 34. Peter Fredrick Rothermel, *The Pioneers* or *The Western Emigrants.* 1849. Engraving, 4" x 6". Engraved by John Sartain, possibly after a lost painting. Illustrated in *The Opal*, 1849. University of South Carolina Library.

immediate foreground remained the same, there are some subtle shifts in their expressions. For instance, in the lithograph the faces appear to be rounded and slightly enlarged, and the harsh manly face of the guide at left tying his shoe is more visible. In the painting the guide's face is obscured, making him appear more youthful, and his crude expression that appears in both the preparatory drawing and the print was eliminated **(Figure 31)**. The face of Rebecca Boone was subtly refined, as was that of the pioneer, Flanders Callaway. There was a slight, but perceptible softening, of Callaway's face from the print and the preparatory drawing to the final state of the painting **(Figure 32)**.

The artist made numerous changes in the figures behind this lead phalanx to emphasize the earnestness and character of Boone's party. Notably, both the position and gaze of the female figure behind Rebecca Boone, perhaps intended to represent one of Boone's daughters, was considerably shifted. In the print she looks to the left, in the painting to the right. A male head between her and Rebecca and the cheery face of a youth holding an ax on his shoulder, absent in the print, were added to fill the compositional triangle whose apex is

Rebecca's head, and to suggest additional pioneer types. Indeed, the figure with the ax was indebted to Peter Frederick Rothermel's 1849 print *The Pioneers* or *The Western Emigrants* **(Figure 34)**.[123] To the left of Rebecca's head another male carrying a rifle was added, and adjacent to him the silhouette of a man wielding a whip on a pack animal was moved up from the right background in the print. His dramatic gesture is vividly outlined against the bright Kentucky sky. In the distance, other figures with cattle were moved from the right side of the composition in the print to the left side in the painting, and, reduced in size, suggest a more numerous band of pioneers.

It was in the landscape background that Bingham made the most significant changes to enhance the typological symbolism of his picture. In the background the clear, serene sky seen in the lithograph was replaced with the dark clouds of a storm. At the center, just above the famed Gap in the Cumberland Mountains, the dark clouds appear to part to the left and right, allowing a burst of brilliant light to flood the picture from the distance. The single bird soaring in the sky on an even, straight course is modified in the final version and tips its wings to fly lower just over the band of pioneers as a kind of divine harbinger of progress.[124] The broad, light-filled valley in the early version is replaced by a dark, stormy valley with high beetling cliffs framing the pioneer's advance. Unlike the moderate sized mountains in the lithograph, the sheer rock walls in the painting sharply define the dark narrow gap through the mountains.

In revising the dark mountain valley Bingham evoked emotions remarkably similar to the sublime word picture described in Filson's text:

> *These mountains are in the wilderness…[and] are of*
> *great length and breadth and, not far distant from each*

other. Over them nature hath formed passes less different than might be expected from the view of such huge piles. The aspect of these cliffs is so wild and horrid, that it is impossible to behold them without terror. The spectator is apt to imagine that nature had formerly suffered some violent convulsion; and that these are the dismembered remains of the dreadful shock; the ruins not of Persepolis or Palmyra, but of the world![125]

The horrific setting described by Filson is expressed visually by landscape forms that owe a debt to prints by Salvator Rosa and to Thomas Cole's later adaptions of Rosa's style of the sublime.[126] An equally vivid biblical text that would have been commonly understood in Bingham's period is the 23rd Psalm, "yea though I walk through the valley of the shadow of death, I will fear no evil . . . ." Its applicability as a typological reference to the passage of the Israelites would have held special resonance for viewers of Bingham's picture reflecting on the ordeal of earlier American pioneers venturing through a dark defile into hostile territory. The profile of the looming cliff above and to the left of the party, and particularly the contrived rock formation above the head of Flanders Callaway, the figure just to the right of Boone, indicate that Bingham, like most of the major artists of his period, was well acquainted with the idea of emblematic personification of nature.[127] The hideous, menacing expression of these anthropomorphic rocks underscores the "wild and horrid terror" of the scene. Their dramatic countenances add impressively to the foreboding dark valley seething with unseen dangers through which the pioneers emerge into the dramatic light of the foreground.

In the foreground the concept of nature as a vitalistic and living force that pioneers must endure, or, if possible, conquer, is further amplified by several important revisions that Bingham made to complete the final state of his picture. Chief among these is the addition in the right foreground of a blasted tree that seems to be reeling backward. Its dramatic expression of writhing fear before the coming of the pathfinder is easily comprehended because the "pathfinder" Boone was famed for cutting trees to open roads into frontier lands. The form of the tree is a close imitation of Cole's treatment of blasted trees, particularly the trees at the left in Cole's *View of Schroon Mountain* **(Figure 33)**, which Bingham could have seen at the 1838 exhibition of the National Academy of Design, or the bending tree at the left in Cole's 1839 *Notch of the White Mountains* **(Figure 35)**, which seems especially similar to Bingham's tree.[128] In the background another tree waves its gnarled branches in contorted anthropomorphic gestures, echoing the blasted arboreal persona in the foreground. Here, nature trembles with excitement and dread before the approach of the new American Moses.

In the left and center foreground further changes occurred that subtly but importantly enhanced the meaning of Bingham's picture. These alterations demonstrated his understanding of typological symbolism and his keen awareness of contemporary issues in the New York art world of the early 1850s. When Bingham returned to New York in the summer of 1849 it had been only a little more than a year since Thomas Cole had died. Even though Bingham probably did not see the Memorial Exhibition of Cole's art held at the American Art-Union Building in the spring and summer of 1848, he must have been aware of it and the intense attention focused on Cole as the founder of what many artists hoped would become a national school of landscape painting. The memorial pictures created by his precocious student Frederic Church and by Asher B.

Figure 35. Detail. Thomas Cole, *The Notch of the White Mountains (Crawford Notch)*. 1839. Oil on canvas, 40" x 60 1/2". National Gallery of Art, Washington, D.C. Andrew W. Mellon Fund.

Durand, President of the National Academy of Design, were still fresh in the artistic community's memory. Although there is no conclusive proof that Bingham saw either Church's impressive *To the Memory of Cole* or Durand's more conventional *Kindred Spirits*, it is likely that he would have been aware of their existence, and of Cole's popular and controversial last series *The Cross and the World*.[129]

During the period immediately following Cole's death, a number of artists attempted to emulate and capitalize on the symbolic potential of cruciform imagery, and Bingham was no exception. Careful examination of *Daniel Boone Escorting Settlers Through the Cumberland Gap* reveals that in the left foreground, just above the rocky ledge, the blasted tree that appears in the lithograph was replaced by two tree branches intersecting to form a cross. This might be regarded as coincidence or mere convention were it not for an even more striking evidence of Bingham's introduction of such symbolism that appears directly in front of Boone and his party. Just to the right of Callaway's feet, a curiously exaggerated horizontal root intersects another upright branch to create a deliberate cross. This motif is completely absent in the lithograph, and, I would argue, was deliberately added by Bingham for iconographic value. Importantly, both root and branch are strongly highlighted by the artist emphasizing their presence. The role of these cruciform symbols in the larger typological program of the image will soon become apparent. Clearly, the changes that Bingham made between the first version of his picture in 1851 and the version known today were anything but superficial or meaningless, as Bloch maintained.

In constructing the complex symbolism of his image, Bingham must have relied on multiple texts, just as he used both Christian and classical allusions in formulating the picture's symbolism. Bloch has pointed out that one documented text source for Bingham was Humphrey Marshall's 1824 *History of Kentucky* which was credited by the *Columbia Missouri Statesman* as being the source for Bingham's imagery.[130] Marshall did mention families moving with Boone to the frontier—a crucially important aspect of the symbolism in Bingham's image—but his reference to the migration was extremely brief. There was a more contemporaneous source available to Bingham in John M. Peck's *Life of Daniel Boone*. Peck's 1847 volume contained a passage that appears to be reflected almost literally in the imagery of Bingham's painting.

> . . . the party slowly made their toilsome way amid the shrubs, and over the logs and loose rocks, that accident had thrown into the obscure trail, which they were following, each man kept a sharp look-out, as though danger or a lurking enemy was near. Their garments were soiled and rent, the unavoidable result of long traveling and exposure to the heavy rains that had fallen; for the weather had been stormy and most uncomfortable, and they had traversed a mountainous wilderness for several hundred miles. The leader of the party was of full size, with a hardy, robust, sinewy frame, and keen, piercing hazel eyes, that glanced with quickness at every object as they passed on, not cast forward in the direction they were travelling for signs of an old trail, and in the next moment directed askance into the dense thicket, or into the deep ravine, as if watching for some concealed enemy. The reader will recognize in this man the pioneer Boone, at the head of his companions.[131]

Interestingly, Bingham, like Ranney who also carefully read Peck, deliberately chose to ignore the reference to the party's clothes being "soiled and rent," for reasons that presumably had to do with pictorial conventions of decorum, or in other words avoiding the ignoble depiction of figures who might appear "mean."

Another passage in Peck seems to have particular applicability to the background of Bingham's image:

> At Powell's Valley, through which their route lay, they were joined by five families and forty men all well armed. This accession of strength gave them courage, and the party advanced full of hope and confident of success. The party ...was approaching Cumberland Gap. Seven young men, who had charge of the cattle, had fallen to the rear some five or six miles from the main body, when unexpectedly they were attacked by a party of Indians.[132]

Neither of these passages occurs in the other sources that Bingham might have consulted, lending further credibility to the contention that Peck's recently published narrative was of considerable importance to Bingham.

A key to one level of conceptual meaning in Bingham's painting is the artist's combination of two major events in Boone's penetration into the Indian Territories of Kentucky. In reality, Boone's first attempt in 1773 had ended in tragic failure when Native Americans repelled him and his band, and six settlers were killed, including Boone's son James. A second, successful attempt took place in 1775 when Boone led his family to the newly constructed Fort Boonesborough, and other settlers followed. In Bingham's painting the landscape and sky, with their dark and threatening clouds and the menacing rocky mountain pass, suggest passages in the texts of Peck and Flint referring to the dangers of the first, unsuccessful march, while the vigilant expressions of the lead figures allude to Boone's later reputation as an Indian killer and his frontier stubbornness that enabled him to penetrate Kentucky despite earlier reverses. Yet the depiction of the pioneers also has a level of personal significance because the artist's own family had undergone the usual privations and difficulties in their own trek westward from a plantation in Augusta County, Virginia, to Franklin County, Missouri, in 1819. It would seem natural that Bingham might have included at least some allusion to his own family's migration in his psychological characterization of Boone's family.

There is another even more important level of meaning in the work that addressed popular ideas about America's place in the divine order of history. As Elizabeth Johns noted, by softening the physiognomy of his figures, especially of Boone and his scout, and by ennobling the lead figure of Boone with a youthful facial characterization, Bingham could symbolically replace all the scoundrels, adventurers, opportunists and exploiters who had ventured west with an image that proclaimed the noble meaning of the *nation's* westward expansion by the best Anglo-Saxon classes.[133] As befitted the Whig artist's conservative views the picture represents the process of civilization by all-white pioneers of the middle class. They are farmers, not squatters, removing their entire community to build a permanent agrarian civilization on the Western frontier.

Another deeper level of meaning is evident in the complex symbolism with which Bingham envelops his figures. Bingham was a deeply religious man. As early as 1835 his religious convictions were evident in a letter addressed to his future wife, Elizabeth Hutchison: "If anything merits our chief concern, religion does, not only because we expect it to make us happy in a future life, but because it is the source of our highest enjoyments in this world also."[134] Bingham's familiarity with the typological mode of thinking is unmistakable in a letter in which he describes the arrival of a certain political figure in Washington, who was ". . . as welcome to the citizens of the district [of Columbia] as was Moses to the Israelites of old, while groaning beneath the heavy burthens of their Egyptian Masters."[135]

Typology could not only embrace references to both Old and New Testament figures and events, but in its largest compass was thought to include Classical and modern types as well. For example, the Greek god Prometheus could become in one of Thomas Cole's paintings a type of Christ.[136] It is therefore entirely consistent with a typological mind-set that direct references to classical Greco-Roman figures also could be incorporated into Bingham's image, signifying both formal references to the great art of the past and underscoring contemporary allusions. Thus, Boone strides forth as a figure modeled from prints or casts. The artist had consulted the famed Greek sculpture the *Doryphorus*, although the position of his legs is reversed. Boone, like the ancient god, is clean shaven. Immaculately attired in freshly pressed, unsoiled buckskins Boone is represented with only a modicum of fringe and without Indian beadwork on his clothes or moccasins, his long rifle confidently carried at the ready on his shoulder, just as the Doryphorus carries his spear.

Boone's companion, the guide at left, ties his shoes in the manner of *Jason* or *Cincinnatus*.[137] In associating the heroic frontiersmen with classical gods and heroes Bingham dignified them and self-consciously suggested their links as antitypes, forerunners of his own progressive, republican and Christian civilization. The republican virtue of Cincinnatus would have been especially appealing to the Whig Bingham.[138]

The biblical allusions to Boone and his company are self-evidently typological, for the pathfinder is as a present-day type of Moses confidently leading his chosen people into the promised lands of the West.[139] At his feet and to his side are rude cruciforms, reminding the spectator that unlike the Hebrew prophet Moses, Daniel Boone and his party are the new American chosen people emigrating West to a Promised Land that is specifically Christian.

Boone's wife, Rebecca Boone, behind him on the white horse illustrates Boone's boast that his wife and daughter were the first white women to stand on the banks of the Kentucky River. Like Boone, Rebecca is a figure who resonates with dual meanings and associations. Sitting atop a white horse, a shawl draped around her, and the highest point in the triangular composition, she is a powerful reminder of the Virgin Mary as seen in prints of Raphael's Madonnas or of the Holy Family's flight into Egypt. As such, she becomes the symbol of all courageous pioneering women, just as Boone, as Moses, becomes an archetype for the male pioneer.

Bingham also had a personal reason for emphasizing the role of women and the family in Western settlement. The strength of his own mother in holding together the artist's family after the death of Bingham's father in 1823 would have been one association. More immediate would have been the death of his first wife in 1848, and his remarriage to Eliza Thomas who became the stepmother for his children. Bingham's tribute to pioneer women was made even more explicit in the lithograph which was dedicated "To the Mothers and Daughters of the West."

What is curiously missing in Bingham's painting is any overt reference to the great burning question of the day: slavery.[140] There are no African-Americans in the column of the new American Israelites advancing through the wilderness. In a letter of June 21, 1855, from Independence, Missouri, Bingham indicated what the absence of blacks in the westward movement meant: "Since I have been here I have observed the emigration which is still passing through the Teritory [sic]. The men are thoughtful and silent, and from the fact that they have *no negroes* with them, the inference is reasonable that their influence will be against slavery."[141] Paradoxically, Bingham himself still owned slaves at the time he was painting his picture of Boone's emigration.[142] Bingham's family had always held slaves, yet he was

49

vehemently opposed to the expansion of slave-holding states, and during the late 1850s gradually began to shift his allegiance from being an ardent Whig to becoming by 1860 a unionist and supporter of Abraham Lincoln.[143]

Bingham's opposition to the expansion of slave-owning states was largely due to his Whig aversion to the lower classes of people he identified as supporting the expansion of slavery into the new Western territories. Since Boone and company represent the best classes of American frontier types—settlers creating farms and enterprise on the frontier—it is important that no blacks or slaves are represented as accompanying the party. There may be other reasons why Bingham chose to refer only by omission to this troubling political issue. One of these must be the social context in which Bingham created his picture. It was painted in New York City to be sold to the Art-Union whose audience consisted largely of urban Easterners, most of whom were vehemently opposed to the expansion of slavery.

Bingham's Boone expresses a fundamentally conservative Whig view of the politics of Western expansion, and is also implicitly antislavery, albeit for what might be considered today the wrong reasons, and it can be said to represent a progressive nationalistic perspective that typified the best in Whig ideology of the late 1840s and early 1850s.[144] Perhaps the best indication of this progressive tendency in the picture is the perspective or viewpoint Bingham establishes. Unlike the passive figures in Ranney's painting, in Bingham's picture the observer stands in front of the party advancing from the East. "When the artist placed the observer in the unsettled Kentucky forests to watch the advancement of civilization from the East," Dawn Glanz argues, "he implied that national history was to be viewed from the vantage point of the Western territories."[145]

Bingham's pictorial strategy in controlling the point of view from which the spectator encounters Boone and his company, and the mixture of conservative and progressive political values expressed in the figures of Boone's party with their typological resonances to biblical prophecy and nationalistic consensus about westward migration identifies the unfolding Christian future of the nation with the taking of the West by a few "good" Anglo-Saxon white men and their families.

Bingham remained preoccupied by the subject of Daniel Boone through the 1850s. During that period he repeatedly proposed, but was never able to realize, a large painting of the pathfinder for the Capitol in Washington. The idea of a commission for a work to adorn the Capitol first seems to appear in correspondence during Bingham's visit to Philadelphia in December 1853, about a year after reworking his 1851 picture of Boone. In a letter to Rollins, who was then in Congress as a Missouri representative, Bingham wrote with unusual familiarity, as if such a commission had been under extended discussion earlier: "Of course, the big

picture, in perspective for the rotunda, will secure you all the support which I can give, though I regret that it cannot even amount to a vote."[146] Two years later Bingham again pressed the issue in a letter to Rollins and intimated at a competition with Emanuel Leutze.

What is the chance for a pictorial embellishment in the Capitol? There is no other edifice, of such magnificence, in the Union, which presents such a space of bare walls. If you are not ripe for such a work of art as the emigration of Boone upon a large scale would be, a full length portrait of Washington might do for a beginning. Were I to receive a commission from the state for such work I would be ambitious to render it superior to that which graces the Hall of Representatives at Washington. I should like to present the "Father of his Country," connected with some historical incident that would rival the far famed picture of Leutze.[147]

In 1857 while working in Düsseldorf, Germany, Bingham again renewed the appeal to his old friend Rollins to help him obtain a commission to paint the subject of Boone's emigration for the Capitol. His ambition was to "paint a life size figure of the Emigration of Boone with the expectation of selling it to Congress and deriving also a profit from its exhibition."[148] By October of 1857, while still in Düsseldorf, Bingham pressed the issue, writing to Rollins, "I have a thought of commencing shortly, my contemplated large picture of the 'emigration of Boone' 12 by 18 feet ... I think this subject ... will form a very popular exhibition in the Western States especially, and may thus amply repay me for the labor bestowed upon it."[149] He never began the large picture, however, perhaps because he was uncertain of the outcome of such an endeavor.

By July of 1858 Bingham was evidently becoming increasingly anxious about securing the long-sought commission for a large painting in the Capitol, for he wrote to Rollins that he would travel to Washington "and enter the list of competitors for an order for a national picture. Leutze expects to leave here for the U.S. with *such an object in view* during the approaching fall."[150] Bingham complained that Leutze "has for some time been an applicant and the encouragement he has received from individuals most likely to control these Art affairs in the Capitol, renders his chance, at present, much better than mine."[151] Because of his proximity to Leutze who was working in Düsseldorf at the same time, Bingham was extremely well informed about the prospects of receiving such a commission. He wrote to Rollins that he received information about the proposed painting for the Capitol from "an intimate acquaintance of Leutze, who gives it to me without being questioned, not dreaming that I am indulging similar aspirations."[152] Bingham knew that Leutze had been indirectly assured by Captain Montgomery Meigs that he would receive the $10,000 commission for a painting to be placed in a stairway in the House of Representatives. Nonetheless, Bingham declared to Rollins:

> As there is yet no work of Art in the Capitol, properly illustrative of the history of the West, it seems to me that a western artist with a western subject should receive especial consideration from this Committee, and also from Congress in the first appropriations which may hereafter be made for such works.
>
> I would be willing to present to a committee authorized to contract for such a work, a small and complete study for the emigration of Boone, or any other subject of equal interest, for their approval, and if they should approve it contract to finish it upon a large scale, to be again subject to their approval before receiving pay for the picture. . . . I will not permit Leutze or any person out of my own family to know any thing of my aims in this matter . . . .[153]

In spite of these efforts Bingham did not receive a commission to paint the Capital stairway with a "western subject by a western artist." In July 1861 Leutze began painting *Westward the Course of Empire Takes its Way*, where Daniel Boone's pioneer role opening the West of Kentucky three quarters of a century earlier was subordinated to a new vision of the nation expanding its empire all the way to the Pacific Ocean. After the Civil War Bingham never again returned to the subject of Daniel Boone.

Figure 36. Carl Wimar, *The Abduction of Daniel Boone's Daughter by the Indians*. 1853.
Oil on canvas, 40" x 50". Washington University Gallery of Art, St. Louis. Gift of John T. Davis.

CHAPTER VII

Sex, Violence, and Martyrdom in Carl Wimar's
The Abduction of Daniel Boone's Daughter by the Indians

At the same time as Ranney and Bingham were reviving the myth of Daniel Boone, the abduction and attempted rape of Daniel Boone's daughter also became a popular theme for artists. The fashionable literary genre of "captivity narratives" exploited hatred of Indians, and, as a major subtext, they further capitalized on anxieties about sexual relationships between white women and Indian men. Because of pervasive racist attitudes, the idea of contacts between whites and Indians was taboo, especially when it involved white women. The traditional religious symbolism of violent martyrdom could be effectively transformed to represent white fears of capture by Indians. Thomas Cole painted several pictures based on James Fenimore Cooper's novel *The Last of the Mohicans*, which captivated the emotions of his audience with this titillating subject. With westward expansion at its height in the 1850s the popularity of captivity narratives also peaked, and Karl Bodmer and Carl Wimar capitalized on this fashionable interest with pictures whose meaning were closely connected to the popularity of the Boone theme.

Around 1851 Karl Bodmer was commissioned by a French publishing company to produce a series of prints for a volume entitled the *Annals of the United States Illustrated—The Pioneers*.[154] Bodmer had achieved renown as a Western artist for his colorful depictions of Indian life along the Missouri River after he traveled in the West with Prince Maximilian of Weid from 1832-1834. Several images in the series were intended to illustrate the life of Daniel Boone, but only two were completed. Both were classic captivity pictures: *The Abduction of the Daughters of Boone and Callaway* and *The Deliverance of the Daughters of D. Boone and Callaway* (**Figures 37, 38**). Because Bodmer was in poor health and pressed to complete other commissions, he hired the young Jean-François Millet to assist him in drawing the series. When the publisher called unannounced at Bodmer's studio to examine the artist's progress in completing the images he was very annoyed to find the unknown Millet working on them. According to legend the publisher

immediately canceled the contract. Only four of the one hundred plates that had been planned were executed, but before Bodmer destroyed the stones, he pulled a small number of impressions.

In creating his lithograph of *The Abduction of the Daughters of Boone and Callaway*, Bodmer relied on John M. Peck's recently published *Life of Daniel Boone*. Portions of Peck's text were excerpted in the lengthy captions for the two lithographs that appeared in both English and French. Peck's book contained an extensive and detailed description of the captivity of Boone and Callaway's daughters that embellished the event, even down to providing a spine tingling comparison of the lurking Indians with the "noiseless and stealthy serpent":

> On the 14th of July, 1776, Betsey Callaway, her sister Frances, and Jemima Boone, a daughter of Captain [Daniel] Boone, the last two about fourteen years of age, carelessly crossed the river opposite to Boonesborough, in a canoe, at a late hour of the afternoon. The trees and shrubs on the opposite bank were thick, and came down to the water's edge; the girls, unconscious of the danger, were playing and splashing the water with paddles, until the canoe, floating with the current, drifted near the shore. Five stout Indians lay there concealed, one of whom, noiseless and stealthy as the serpent crawled down the bank until he reached the rope that hung from the bow, turned its course up stream, and in a direction to be hidden from the view of the fort. The loud shrieks of the captured girls were heard, but too late for their rescue.[155]

The caricature-like Indian faces and the innocent, virginal appearance of the women makes transparent the sexual innuendo of Bodmer's image as a classic example of the captivity theme.

The second lithograph, *Deliverance of the Daughters of D. Boone and Callaway* (**Figure 38**) is probably the work of Millet because of its dark tangled forest interior that became the hallmark of his Barbizon style.[156] The text accompanying

53

Figure 37. Karl Bodmer and Jean-François Millet, *The Abduction of the Daughters of Boone and Callaway.* 1852. Lithograph, 17" x 22 2/16". Washington University Gallery of Art, St. Louis. Transferred from Special Collections. Gift of Mrs. Charles W. Bryan, Jr.

Figure 38. Karl Bodmer and Jean-François Millet, *Deliverance of the Daughters of D. Boone and Callaway.* 1852.
Lithograph, 17" x 22 15/16". Washington University Gallery of Art, St. Louis. Transferred from Special Collections.
Gift of Mrs. Charles W. Bryan, Jr.

the print in the margin was again excerpted from Peck.

Next morning by daylight we were on the track, but found they had totally prevented our following them, by walking some distance apart through the thickest canes they could find… . [Boone] overtook them just as they were kindling a fire to cook… . Four of us fired, and all rushed on them… The place was very thick with canes, and being so much elated on recovering the three little broken-hearted girls, prevented our making a further search.[157]

The joyous embraces at the right and the dramatic silhouette of the wildly gesturing figures in firelight at the left expresses the relief of Boone's party. Like a modern cinematic thriller they would have appealed to a European audience eager for images of sex and violence on the faraway American frontier.

The usefulness of Indians as a device for heightening the emotional impact of the Boone legend was key to the imagery of Carl Wimar, the young German-born artist whose family had settled in St. Louis. Wimar painted several pictures related to the Daniel Boone theme, exploiting tales of Boone's encounters with hostile Native Americans. Wimar may have seen Bodmer's lithographs of the Abductions of Boone's and Callaway's Daughters in Bodmer's Cologne studio. However, Wimar's ambition was to create large-scale history paintings in the grand style, and whatever he may have absorbed from the Bodmer/Millet lithographs was overshadowed by the influence of his mentor Emanuel Leutze. While studying art in Düsseldorf Wimar began a series of paintings of Western subjects that he hoped would sell well in St. Louis.

All the major paintings from this early period of

Figure 39. Artist unknown, *Capture of Boone's Daughter*. In Cecil B. Hartley's *The Life of Daniel Boone, The Great Western Hunter and Pioneer*. (New York: Lovell, Coryell & Company, 1859). The St. Louis Mercantile Library Association.

Wimar's career dealt with confrontation and conflict between Native Americans and settlers, according to Wimar scholar Joseph D. Ketner.[158] By the end of his first year of study Wimar had completed two major works derived from accounts of Daniel Boone. Wimar wrote to his family in St. Louis, "Indian and American topics in general seem to be especially well-liked here, and there is nobody else who does them."[159] In order to facilitate his paintings of Western life in America, Wimar had his family send him Indian artifacts and clothes in which he dressed his German models to achieve the desired "primitive" effect.

One of the first subjects Wimar painted in 1853 after arriving in Düsseldorf was *The Discovery of Boone's Encampment* **(Figure 40)**. It was derived from his reading John M. Peck's account of Boone's life with its vivid description of Indian warfare and surprise attack on settler's encampments.

It was now known that parties of hostile Indians were prowling through the forests, that their spies were watching each station . . . .

The Indian method of besieging a fort, village, or even a single cabin in peculiar. they are seldom seen in considerable force. They lie concealed in the bushes and weeds, or behind stumps and trees; they waylay the path, or the field in a stealthy manner cut off any persons that pass in their way. They will crawl on the ground, or assume and imitate the noise and appearance of swine, bears, or any other animal, in the dark . . . . Indians very seldom fight when exposed in the open field. They take to the trees or other objects for protection. They are not brave, but cunning and wary; not cool and calculating, but sly and treacherous. Such was the enemy that assaulted the feeble garrisons of Kentucky.[160]

Unfortunately, Wimar's painting is now known only through a poor reproduction.[161] Unlike Ranney and Bingham, Wimar's approach was not to show Boone directly, but to concentrate on events surrounding his career and family. Hence *The Discovery of Boone's Encampment* depicted three Indians treated like pieces of neo-classical sculpture, and attired in all the authentic costuming and accessories of Native American culture that Wimar could collect from his family in St. Louis. Wimar's Indians are depicted as repulsive characters, their expressions distorted by rage. The idea for the composition with the Indians stealthily spying on Boone's camp from a high bluff was not Wimar's invention. There is little doubt that Wimar's work was influenced by George Caleb Bingham's painting *The Concealed Enemy*, which was included in American Art-Union exhibition in New York in 1845 **(Figure 41)**.[162] The two compositions are remarkably similar, but the expressions of Wimar's "treacherous" Indians recalls Peck's dramatic account.

Figure 40. Photograph of Carl Wimar's lost painting *The Discovery of Boone's Encampment.* 1853. Oil on Canvas. In Perry Rathbone, *Charles Wimar 1828-1862: Painter of the Indian Frontier.* (St. Louis: St. Louis Art Museum, 1946), page 57.

Figure 41. George C. Bingham, *The Concealed Enemy.* 1845.
Oil on canvas, 29 1/4" x 36 1/2". Stark Museum of Art, Orange, Texas.

Figure 42. Emanuel Leutze, *The Vikings First Landing in America*. 1845. Oil on canvas, Kunstmuseum Düsseldorf. Loan of Mr. Horst Volmer, Remsheid.

Figure 43. Carl Wimar, *The Abduction of Daniel Boone's Daughter by the Indians*. 1853. Charcoal and sepia on paper, 36" x 44". The St. Louis Art Museum.

Another aspect of the Boone legend—captivity—appeared in Wimar's 1853 depiction of *The Abduction of Daniel Boone's Daughter by the Indians* (**Figure 36**). Wimar's reading of Peck's book and knowledge of Bodmer's lithographs may have suggested the subject. Another source for the image, Ketner argues in an unpublished article, may have been Daniel Bryan's *Mountain Muse*, which contained several verses that seem to evoke the libidinous imagery that resonates in Wimar's picture.[163] The subject proved to be so successful that Wimar completed at least four versions of the subject, three of which are extant. The composition of Wimar's painting was influenced, not by Bodmer's lithographs, but by the example of Wimar's neighbor in Düsseldorf, Emanuel Leutze. Leutze's historical painting *The Vikings First Landing in America*, painted in 1845 (**Figure 42**), was carefully studied by the young Wimar who adapted both the triangular composition of Leutze's main figures and recast the gestures of the Vikings for his Indian protagonists.

The earliest version of Wimar's *Abduction of Boone's Daughter* was completed by the end of the artist's first year in Düsseldorf. Wimar simplified Peck's account by depicting Jemima Boone alone in her canoe, without her sisters and Callaway's daughter, Betsey. She is shown kneeling in the boat with her hands folded in prayer for mercy from her three captors, two of whom search anxiously for signs of pursuing settlers. In what must have been the most offensive figure in the image for Wimar's white audience, the third Indian holding the canoe gazes lasciviously at the fair-skinned woman.

It is the posture and expression of "the high soul'd Jemima Boone" that is the key to unlocking the meaning of Wimar's painting, and its contribution to the symbolism of captivity images. Characteristically, for a mid-19th century American artist, Wimar turned to religious iconography for the figure of Jemima. Through the subtle conversion process encouraged by the idea of typology, Boone's daughter was transformed into the type of a Christian martyr. In this case the figure is Mary Magdalene, whose kneeling gesture at the foot of Christ's cross was well-known in Counter Reformation and Baroque painting. The haggard Magdalene prototype for the figure is most evident in the preparatory study for the *Abduction of Daniel Boone's Daughter* in which Jemima Boone's hair, dress and features are depicted as rough and unkempt (**Figure 43**). The final figure of Jemima in the painting is one in which her sensual beauty and potential for salvation are combined with powerful allusions to her sexual desirability.

Jemima's pose of kneeling supplication is the key to the symbolic resonances of Wimar's image. On one level she is pleading for mercy from her captors while praying for rescue from the pagan Indians who have abducted her. Her dramatic gesture metaphorically signifies hope for redemption from the sexual violation she expects to suffer at the hands of the Indians. As Wimar represents her, the chaste Jemima is an emblem of feminine virtue in Euro-American society, at risk both physically and morally in the wilderness. Provocatively falling from her shoulder, the white fabric of her blouse reveals the sensual flesh of her breast and shoulder. Ketner argues that the triangular form of the brown drapery falling across her arms hints at the shape of female genitalia, while the brilliant red drapery at her knees hints at the bloody prospect of sexual violation. The gaze of the Indian holding the boat further emphasizes Jemima's forbidden appeal.[164]

Like Wimar's contemporaneous depiction of Indians spying on Boone's camp, the abduction picture is a revelation of mid-19th-century American notions about the sexual promiscuousness of Native Americans and their treatment of white women. Commonly captivity narratives perpetuated the myth that Indians raped their female captives. However, the woodland Indians of Boone's period preferred to ransom their captives, adopt them into the tribe, or sell them in Canada as slaves.[165] Wimar's *Abduction* played upon this stereotype, and provided another instance for self-righteous Americans that their Christian way of life was superior to that of the immoral Indians. Numerous variants were created during the 1850s and 1860s from Wimar's image, beginning with its appearance as a woodcut in Cecil B. Hartley's 1859 *Life of Daniel Boone* (**Figure 39**).[166] They perpetuated for several generations the unequivocal implications of Wimar's image: if Indians violated settlers, especially women, the morally superior whites were justified in annihilating them.

Figure 44. Emanuel Leutze, *Westward the Course of Empire Takes Its Way*. 1861.
Oil on canvas, 33 1/4" x 43 3/8". National Museum of American Art, Washington, D.C. Bequest of Sara Carr Upton.

CHAPTER VIII

The Typology of Manifest Destiny:
Marginalizing Daniel Boone in Emanuel Leutze's
Westward the Course of Empire Takes Its Way

anifest Destiny was the ideological creed that powered and justified American expansion into the Western wilderness in the decade before the Civil War. Yet, ironically, this notion which was vital to the emergence of Daniel Boone as a symbol of national expansion led to the eventual eclipse of Boone as an emblem for pioneers establishing a transcontinental empire. In what was perhaps the single most important representation of the idea of Manifest Destiny, Emanuel Leutze's mural for the Capitol, *Westward the Course of Empire Takes Its Way* **(Color Plate 4, Figure 44)**, Daniel Boone was not the central protagonist, as Bingham had planned to depict him. Instead Leutze relegated Boone to the margin of the composition as a "prophet" whose labors in the Eastern wilderness had foretold the nation's redemption of its promised land in the Far West.

In order to understand this final phase in the visual representations of Boone, it is essential to grasp the subtle changes that the ideology of Manifest Destiny dictated for the Boone persona. The belief that the nation had a divinely ordained destiny had religious foundations in the 17th and 18th century Puritan conviction that Americans were engaged in a great civilizing mission—a sacred errand into the wilderness.[167] The merging of ideas of biblical typology and national destiny strengthened this belief so that by the mid-1840s it could be used to justify even the most self-serving ambitions for territorial conquest and appropriation, such as the Mexican War of 1847-1848 and the subsequent annexation of Texas, California, and other Western territories.

Manifest Destiny invoked the idea that the nation itself was the instrument of a divine order of history. In the late 18th and early 19th century, this providential force was believed to be revealed through great men like Daniel Boone. By the 1850s, the increasing power of nationalism shifted the emphasis from divine intervention operating through the heroism of a single man to larger collective forces embodied in the nation. The idea of Providence, the direct intervention of divinity in human affairs manifested in special individuals like Daniel Boone, was replaced by the belief that divine will manifested itself through the collective

body of the nation, through "types" who could symbolize a broader consensus about national destiny. Above all, the subtext operating in the typology of Manifest Destiny concealed an imperative to establish an entrepreneurial culture from the Atlantic to the Pacific.

The phrase "Manifest Destiny" itself was not coined until 1845 by the New York newspaper editor John L. O'Sullivan, who declared in the *New York Morning News* that "[The American claim] is by right of our manifest destiny to overspread and possess the whole of the continent which Providence has given us for the development of ... a noble young empire...."[168] By 1854 even such a recent emigrant as the German-born intellectual Philip Schaff declared that:

> When history shall have erected its central stage of action on the magnificent theater of the new world, the extreme ends of the civilized world will be brought together by the power of steam and electricity, the wonderful achievements of modern science, the leveling influences of the press and public opinion, and the more silent, but deeper and stronger workings of the everlasting Gospel. Then [will come] the millennium of righteousness. This [is] the distinctive mission of the American nation, to represent the compact, well defined and yet world embracing. As the children of pilgrims, and of the sturdy Puritans, whose descendants are the chief pioneers in our western States and territories, we are the nation of the future. [We] must be magnificent as Niagara Falls, lofty as the Rocky Mountains, vast as our territory, far-reaching as the highways of commerce. The first Adam was the type and prophecy of the second Adam [Christ]; the very name of Abraham pointed to the Messianic blessings that should flow from [our] seed upon the nations of the earth.[169]

The merging of notions of biblical typology and the rhetoric of Manifest Destiny reached its height at mid-century. A key example of this is found in the introduction to C. W. Dana's volume promoting westward migration, entitled *The Garden of the World, or the Great West*. "The Land of Promise, and the Canaan of our time, is the region which, commencing on the slope of the Alleghanies [sic], broadens grandly over the vast prairies ... [to] kiss the golden shores of El Dorado."[170] The explicit linking of the American land of promise with the biblical Canaan is typical of the typological mode of thinking that eagerly divined or devised symbolic linkage between the biblical past, the ambitions of the present, and the prospect of a glorious future.

The most prolix promoter of Manifest Destiny was William Gilpin, who wrote during the 1850s when the divine imperative sustaining the "mission" of American expansion seemed indisputable.[171] Gilpin extolled the moral virtue of such expansion, as in the following passage:

> *The untransacted destiny of the American people is to subdue the continent—to rush over this vast field to the Pacific Ocean—to animate the many hundred millions of its people, and cheer them upward … to establish a new order in human affairs … to regenerate superannuated nations—to change darkness into light … to teach old nations a new civilization—to confirm the destiny of the human race—to carry the career of mankind to its*

culminating point—to cause stagnant people to be reborn—to perfect science … to unite the world in a social family—to absolve the curse that weights down humanity, and to shed blessings round the world!

> *Divine task! Immortal mission! Let us tread fast and joyfully the open trail before us! Let every American heart open wide for patriotism to grow undiminished, and confide with religious faith in the sublime and prodigious destiny of his well-loved country.*[172]

Central to the idea of Manifest Destiny was the belief that God had mandated an American Empire from the Atlantic to the Pacific— that the nation would mediate between Europe and Asia. Behind this extraordinary declaration lay a belief that "Nature is benign and graceful throughout her whole scheme." It was in America, as Gilpin put it, that "the pre-eminently divine gifts had been vouchsafed to the *American people* by God *through nature*."[173] Gilpin could often be fanatical, as in the following passage:

Figure 45. John Gast, *American Progress* or *Manifest Destiny*. 1872.
Oil on Canvas, 12 3/4" x 16 3/4". N & R Enterprises, Inc., Hampton, New Hampshire.

A glance of the eye thrown across the North American continent . . . reveals an extraordinary landscape. It displays immense forces, characterized by order, activity and progress. . . .

Farms, cities, states, public works, define themselves, flash into form, accumulate, combine and harmonize.

The American realizes that "Progress is God." He clearly recognizes and accepts the continental mission of his country and his people.[174]

Gilpin stated the ultimate economic purpose of this imperial program: "I discern ... a new power, the *people occupied in the wilderness*, engaged at once in extracting from its recesses the omnipotent element of *gold coin*; and disbursing it immediately for the *industrial* conquest of the world."[175]

The single most comprehensive image expressing the ideology of Manifest Destiny was John Gast's *American Progress* or *Manifest Destiny* **(Figure 45)**. It was created in 1872 as an advertisement for George A. Crofutt's book *New Overland Tourist and Pacific Coast Guide*.[176] Gast's naive painting summarized in one picture all of the successive phases of the establishment of the transcontinental empire. At the center floats the allegorical figure of Progress—the "Star of Empire"—posed midway between light and darkness, the East on the right and the West with the Pacific Ocean on the left. She is a secularized angel whose wings are replaced by fluttering robes. In her right hand she holds a "school book," the "emblem of education and the testimonial of our national enlightenment," while her left hand strings a telegraph wire to connect East and West with instant communication. In the sky at left, storm clouds retreat toward the Rocky Mountains. Behind the allegorical symbol of progress, a warm, golden light falls upon the various human protagonists and technological instruments of progress.

In the foreground a Boone-like figure in a coonskin hat with a rifle at the ready leads an explorer on horseback and a

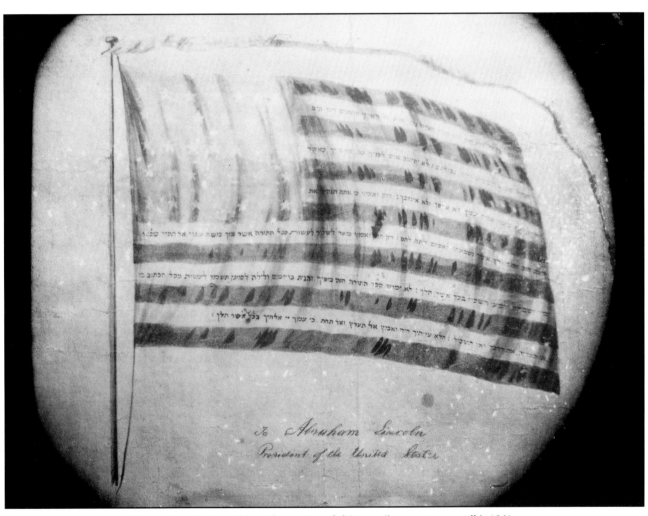

Figure 46. Abraham Kohn, *The Star Spangled Banner* (lost painting on silk). 1861. Photograph. Collection K.A.M. Temple Isaiah Israel, Chicago.

Figure 47. Emanuel Leutze, *Westward the Course of Empire Takes Its Way*. 1862. Water-glass painting, 240" x 360". United States Capitol, Washington, D.C. Photograph: Architect of the Capitol.

Figure 48. Robert W. Weir, *"Westward the Star of the Empire Takes Its Way" in Progress at the National Capitol by E. Leutze*. 1861-62. Ink on paper, 5" x 7 1/2". Arthur J. Phelan, Jr., Chevy Chase, Maryland.

prospector with a shovel. Following the vanguard of civilization are farmers with livestock, plows, and the log cabin homestead. Above the agriculturalists are the stagecoach, the covered wagon, and the pony express rider who suggest earlier modes of transportation; while, to the right, three railroads with trains moving west allude to the planned, but then as yet unrealized, Central, Southern and Northern Pacific Railroads. At extreme right is the gleaming metropolis of New York, including the Brooklyn Bridge, begun but not yet completed at the time the picture was painted. At the left Indians, buffalo, wild horses, and bears are retreating westward. As Crofutt put it, "The Indians ... turn their despairing faces toward the setting sun, as they flee from the presence of the wondrous vision. The 'Star' is *too much for them*."[177] Gast's painting symbolizes in one concise image the self-serving ideology of westward expansion, its allegorical figure floating across the sky making explicit the conflation of sacred and secular in the visual rhetoric of Manifest Destiny.

Numerous examples of the ideology of Manifest Destiny were to be found in literature and in the expansionist political rhetoric of the antebellum period. A remarkable, unpublished image in which the concept of typology and Manifest Destiny are explicitly articulated is a hand-painted American flag on silk that was presented to President-elect Abraham Lincoln on the eve of the Civil War **(Figure 46)**. It was created by Abraham Kohn, a prominent member of Chicago's Jewish community and a prosperous haberdasher, as well as the Republican City Clerk of Chicago and a leading Abolitionist.[178] Lincoln met Kohn during a visit to Chicago shortly after his election in 1860, and the two became friends. Kohn immediately began work on the flag, which showed a union with 35 stars. On the bars he painted in Hebrew letters excerpts from the 4th through the 9th verses of the first chapter of Joshua.

The flag was received by Lincoln in February 1861 in Springfield, Illinois, before he departed for inauguration in Washington. Although the actual flag is lost, its image survives in a glass plate photograph. While the Hebrew inscription is virtually indecipherable in the slightly out-of-focus photograph, fortunately the Springfield *Daily Illinois State Journal* on February 7, 1861, carried a lengthy commentary on the flag, a note which made absolutely explicit the typological associations with contemporary events symbolized by the biblical verses.

Kohn's flag was a classic and unprecedented instance of a painted counterpart to the verbal rhetoric of the Puritan sermon of woe, known as the Jeremiad, that Sacvan Bercovitch and Perry Miller have discussed as a key to the power of typology to motivate behavior.[179] The *State Journal's* transcription of the verses on the flag's bar field (the actual words painted on the flag were indicated in bold type) is profoundly indicative of how such symbolism functioned in defining the parallels between biblical prophecy and contemporary feelings of social and political urgency as the Union was beginning to disintegrate on the eve of the Civil War. The printed texts read:

> 4. *From the wilderness and the Lebanon even unto the great river, the river Euphrates, all the land of the Hittites; and unto the great sea toward the going down of the sun, shall be your coast.*
>
> 5. ***There shall not any man be able to stand before thee,*** *all the days of this life; as I was with Moses, so I will be with thee; I will not fail thee, nor forsake thee.*
>
> 6. ***Be strong and of good courage,*** *for unto this people shalt thou divide for an inheritance the land, which I swear unto their fathers to give them.*
>
> 7. ***Only be thou strong and very courageous*** *that thou may observe to do according to all the law, which Moses, my servant commanded thee; turn not from it to the right hand or to the left, that thou mayest prosper whithersoever thou goest.*
>
> 8. *This book of the law shall not depart out of thy mouth, but thou shalt mediate thereon day and night, that thou mayest observe to do according to all that is written therein; further thou shalt make thy way prosperous, and then thou shalt have good success.*
>
> *Have not I commanded thee:* ***Be strong and of good courage: be not afraid, neither be thou dismayed;*** *for the Lord thy God is with thee whithersoever thou goest.*
>
> *The picture was surrounded by a gilt frame, and accompanied by a letter from the Donor Abr. Kohn, Esq. City Clerk of Chicago,... to which was annexed the following:*
>
> **NOTES**
> *1. Wilderness—the sandy soil of Florida*
> *2. Lebanon—the forests of Maine*
> *3. Land of the Hittites—the land of the Indians*
> *4. Going down of the sun—California and Oregon*
> *5. Moses—Washington*
> **6. The Law—the Constitution of the United States**
>
> *Mr. Lincoln politely received the picture.*[180]

The review makes specific the equation of geographical places such as Florida and Maine with biblical types like the wilderness and Lebanon through which the tribes of Israel wandered, while the Hittites are equated as types of the Indians, the biblical phrase "going down of the sun" becomes a type of California and Oregon, Moses is a father of the nation like Washington, and the Hebrew laws are equivalent types of the Constitution. Kohn's flag indicates to what lengths the concepts of typology had penetrated middle class intellectual life, even that of a recent Jewish emigrant in remote Chicago.

Perhaps nowhere in 19th-century American art was the typology of Manifest Destiny more exultantly realized than in Emanuel Leutze's huge 20 by 30 foot mural painting *Westward the Course of Empire Takes Its Way* **(Figure 47)**, created for a stairway in the United States House of Representatives.[181] The painting reproduced here **(Color Plate 4, Figure 44)** is one of two small studies in oil on canvas for the staircase mural. Leutze's picture was an official icon of national expansion (the title of the mural was sometimes simply given as *Westward Ho!*)—a visual symbol of the national ambition for a transcontinental empire.

For Americans of Leutze's generation, the conquest of the West marked the fulfillment of Columbus's dream of reaching the riches of the East by sailing West. The title of Leutze's picture comes from Bishop George Berkeley's poem "On the Prospect of Planting Arts and Learning in America" written between 1729 and 1731:

> *Westward the course of empire takes its way;*
> *The first four acts already past,*
> *A fifth shall close the drama with the day:*
> *Time's noblest offspring is the last.*

A Boston reviewer reflected, "We can only wish that [Berkeley] had been able, as he penned this line, to foresee how deeply it was destined to sink into the minds of future generations, to become the watchword of a mighty policy," and he continued "how it was to appear to the eyes of a painter as he journeyed out to Pike's Peak ... to gather there the gorgeous colorings and mature the fancies by which to fasten it upon the walls of the Capitol of a great nation as the teacher of the chosen men of our Legislature."[182] In July 1861, as Leutze was beginning his work, the writer for *The Home Journal* noted that "The subject is treated in a purely imaginative style ... surrounded by an emblematical border, which serves as a prelude to it."[183]

The art critic Henry Tuckerman commented on the didactic purpose of the Capitol mural which "should be made to subserve the purpose of illustrating the history of our country." The importance of such an image, Tuckerman asserted, was as "a book of art whose illuminated pages, bound in the enduring marble of the nation's Capitol, shall forever lie open for the perusal of the generations that are to come after us . . . ."[184] In a long article, excerpted in his 1867 *Book of the Artists*, Tuckerman extolled the sentiments of Leutze's picture:

> *An emigrant party, travel-stained and weary, who for long weeks have toiled on in the face of formidable difficulties over the vast plains on the hither side of the Rocky Mountains, have reached near sundown the point . . . from which they catch the first glimpse of the vast Pacific slope—their land of promise. El Dorado, indeed, for earth and sky and mountain peaks are bathed in the golden glow of the setting sun. On the left of the picture, leagues away in the dim distance, a faint line on the horizon reveals the western ocean . . . . Above, on the highest point*

of rock some of the western-bound pilgrims are planting the Stars and Stripes.[185]

Leutze's work was hailed as visual prophecy by the critic for the *Boston Transcript* who proclaimed, "[Leutze] has sketched a noble epic in colors—a winged word—voiceless, but unmistakably 'a handwriting on the wall' of true American genius," and he continued, "in these dark days of trial, we felt the beauty of the whole marvelous production almost as a prophetic conviction that the idea of our 'manifest destiny' should not perish."[186] The same critic rhapsodized: "It is, beyond question, the most thoroughly *national* picture; the purest revelation of what is in the minds of us all—our cherished hopes and habits of thought. It flashes upon the soul in an instant, and an hour's study deepens the impression."[187]

Leutze created drama in his composition by dividing the scene into realms of light on the left, where the figures of the overland party, who have struggled through a dark valley, reach the golden sunset light at the right—conventional symbol for the beckoning land of California. The ascending axis formed by the pioneers at the right culminates in the family group at the center of the composition. This group, a mother with an infant child and her husband in a coonskin hat, gesture excitedly toward the Pacific Ocean. The pose of this central group was intended to be read as a type of the Holy Family on the Flight into Egypt conflated with the New Israelites going to the New Canaan of California. The coonskin hat was a symbol associated with David Crockett, a frontiersman like Boone long identified with the stereotype of the West. The domain of the "holy family" is not only geographical but temporal, as the excited critic for the *Boston Transcript* blazed: "The eye follows the finger of the foremost figure, over miles and miles of mountain tops, 'Alp on Alp,' marked by the signal fires of the Indians, into the dim and distant future."[188] The young boy in the red shirt before them was identified as "a type of 'Young America' musing on the future," according to Tuckerman.

Like Moses ascending Mount Pisgah and finally looking out at the Promised Land, many of the toilers coming up the trail are excited by the promise of their redemption, but still unaware of the glowing landscape spread out for the viewer. And just as Moses had brought his people into the Promised Land of Canaan, Leutze's mural symbolized the self-serving conviction that Americans were in fact God's chosen people on a mission to redeem California and Oregon.

Behind these lead figures are other "types"—the "suffering wife," for example, and "a lad who has been wounded, probably in a fight with the Indians."[189] The foreground figures are carefully delineated by age and type. Each bears the marks of his or her place in the stages of life, from the limping youth assisted by an older companion, to the family group in the wagon at right. Every figure contributes an expression of emotion to the overall narrative. Other pairings of mothers with children are glimpsed in the lower right, suggesting that potentially every American family is a "holy family." Even death is present on the march to Paradise in the burial of an old woman at the center right. Leutze was careful to omit this scene in his mural because of the Civil War. It had halted the westward migration, and was, even as he labored to complete the mural, traumatizing the national consciousness with its carnage.

Nature itself becomes a mute witness to the progress of the nation. The rocks in the background of the easel painting appear to echo the triumphant gestures of the pioneers as they strain expectantly toward the golden horizon. Endowing inanimate objects like rocks with human emotions was often considered an indulgence in the "pathetic fallacy" decried by the art critic John Ruskin, but it was also an expressive aesthetic convention that was well understood in mid-19th-century American landscape painting. This natural sign becomes more explicit in the Capitol mural as Leutze configured the large rock just behind the central group to resemble a human face in profile, complete with eye, nose, and mouth formed from the strata of rocks. A flat slab of rock at the top suggests the coonskin hat of the "Joseph" figure in the foreground. This anthropomorphic symbol expressed the idea of vitalistic nature, and was another current of symbolism supporting the all-embracing typology of Leutze's mural.

Leutze was still more explicit with the typological symbolism of his image in the elaborate border of the easel painting, as well as in the "emblematical border" in the mural. Stretching across the bottom like a predella panel in a Renaissance altar painting is a view of San Francisco Bay—the "Golden Gate." The Golden Gate is significant because it had been the ultimate goal of pioneers during the Gold Rush of 1849. Flanking it are medallions of the new American holy men—the explorers Daniel Boone at the left, in a fur collar coat recalled from Chester Harding's images, and William Clark at the right, dressed in the garb of an Indian scout. Leutze's predella landscape is a painted emblem of a mythical land of sublime physical beauty perfectly fitted for the new beginning of American civilization.

Typological associations are further elaborated at the side and top borders, painted to simulate a Gothic relief and filled with emblems and symbolic types. In the center of the upper margin the eagle shields Union and Liberty with his wings, while before them flees the "stealthy savage." Above Boone at the left is the raven who brought bread to Elijah, paired on the opposite side with the dove returning to Noah's ark with an olive branch. Both were considered biblical types of divine intervention. Above the raven is Moses descending from the mountain with the Tablets of the Law, and on the right is Columbus with a globe and compass, symbols of divine guidance. The next pair of medallions, left and right, are a Viking ship sailing toward the New World and the Hebrew spies returning from the

promised land of Canaan with giant grapes of Eschol, symbols of abundance and of the later promise of the Eucharist and the coming of Christ. They are typological symbols foreshadowing the present discovery of America's great riches. The upper left corner depicts the Magi, the Wise Men of the East following the star to the West, while on the right is Hercules with a scroll bearing a part of the motto *ne plus ultra* ("nothing more beyond"). He is dividing the Pillars of Gibraltar to open the path to the Atlantic. The top border has an eagle at center, flanked by an Indian and a mountain lion. The whole ensemble forms a classic visual justification for the imperial American fantasy of a Western empire.[190]

Leutze did not win final congressional approval to begin work on the Capitol mural until June 1861. Leutze's patron, Captain Montgomery C. Meigs, had appealed to Lincoln's new Secretary of War, Simon Cameron, regarding the patriotic value of the project.[191]

> *The people of the country have so responded to the call of their Government that danger to the Capitol [by Southern troops] has now passed away, and . . . the Government by . . . completing its Capitol would now give to the people a welcome assurance of its confidence in its own strength and in the patriotism of its people.*[192]

The mural in the Capitol differs in several important respects from the oil study prepared for Secretary Cameron. By using a more expansive format in the mural Leutze accommodated additional figures and several details that do not appear in the study. An African-American leading a white woman on a donkey in the foreground is the most notable. This figure is missing in the study, for reasons that Patricia Hills has argued had to do with gaining the approval of Secretary Cameron, who opposed the extension of slave-owning into the Western territories.[193]

Another key detail in the mural version that reflects the fervent patriotism of 1861 is the group on the highest peak. One of the figures is about to plant an American flag, confirming that the "Emigration to the West," the title Leutze had originally proposed for his picture, would be a Union one, bound by the lawful Constitution of the nation. If Leutze had been able to fulfill his ambitious plans, he might have painted on the side walls of the staircase "the earlier history of Western Emigration, in illustrations from Boone's adventures [in] the discovery of the valleys of the Ohio, [and] Mississippi."[194] But this did not occur, and Daniel Boone remained at the periphery as a small emblematic medallion in the composition.

Reaction to Leutze's mural was predictably positive, especially in New York papers like the *Evening Post*, edited by the patriotic William Cullen Bryan, which printed Henry Tuckerman's enthusiastic review. In July 1862 the *Atlantic Monthly* published Nathaniel Hawthorne's account of a recent trip to Washington where he had inspected Leutze's mural. Hawthorne asserted,

> *The work will be emphatically original and American, embracing characteristics that neither art nor literature have yet dealt with, and producing new forms of artistic beauty from the natural features of the Rocky-Mountain regions, which Leutze seems to have studied broadly and minutely . . . . It looked full of energy, hope, progress, irrepressible movement onward, all represented in a momentary pause of triumph; and it was most cheering to feel its good augury at this dismal time, when our country might seem to have arrived at such a deadly standstill.*[195]

The complexity of Leutze's image, with its associations of typology and the contemporary issues of slavery, was explicitly acknowledged by the artist in an interview with the critic Anne Brewster who queried the artist about the meaning of his mural.

> *There is a group in the center of your picture—a young Irish woman seated on an ass holding a child—the ass is led by a negro. Did you not mean this group to teach a new gospel to this continent, a new truth which this part of the world is to accept—that the Emigrant and the Freedman are the two great elements which are to be reconciled and worked with? The young, beautiful Irish woman, too, is she not your new Madonna?*
>
> *The artist's face glowed . . . the hard ridges on the brow and cheeks grew soft, and his eyes fairly laughed with joy at my comprehension of his thoughts . . . . I learned afterward that although my interpretation was original so far as I was concerned, it has been made by others and approved by the artist.*[196]

Brewster's interpretation, along with those of other commentators, makes it clear that Leutze's contemporaries understood that the great mural was the creation of Leutze's imagination, a grandiose spectacle of contemporary history—a veritable "book of art framed by the marble permanence of the Capitol." Indeed, Leutze himself recognized the powerful element of idealization in his picture, stating in reference to his work that, "...without a wish to date or localize, or represent a particular event, it is intended to give in condensed form a picture of Western emigration, the conquest of the Pacific slope...."[197]

Only implicitly articulated by contemporary commentaries is the utility of Leutze's representation. It provided a means of assuring, or, at least during the Civil War, with its disintegration of the national consensus, of propping up established social compacts and political agendas. By relying on typology—the notion that there was a continuum between the past, the present, and the future—Leutze attempted to ensure that the cultural values of the dominant middle classes of the Northeast would be maintained. Leutze and his Congressional patrons may have hoped that com-

pleting the transcontinental empire under the ideological auspices of Manifest Destiny could once again provide powerful social cohesion binding the nation together after the Civil War. A great piece of public art at the heart of the Union Capitol would powerfully argue that point.

A surprising insight into the significance of Leutze's painting is provided by a small drawing that Robert W. Weir evidently sketched on the spot as Leutze labored to complete the staircase mural **(Figure 48)**. In a recent study, William H. Truettner has discussed the importance of Weir's sketch. He suggests that Weir's drawing reveals that the process of creating Leutze's mural was analogous to a kind of visual theater of history. For visitors, seeing the mural with its brilliant colors and frenetic action for the first time in 1862 would have had the impact of vicariously creating a visual equivalent for the spectacle of westward emigration, much as the cinema or television might have done in the 20th century.[198]

Weir's drawing recalls the setting of Leutze's work in the Capitol staircase almost as if it were inside a palatial studio. Seated in chairs in the foreground and standing about are spectators admiring and witnessing the progress of the artist at his work. A table with decanters and wine glasses invites these studio visitors to relax with a drink. At the center, one guest holds up a glass as if in salute to the scene and the artist before him. Leutze, like some actor on stage, is on a high scaffold, his back turned to his studio visitors, maulstick in hand, engrossed in the creative moment. Faintly outlined on the wall is the large composition. To the side on a large easel is the preparatory study, or cartoon, for the fresco. It may well be the oil on canvas painting reproduced here. Almost certainly the favored chairs were generally occupied by Congressmen and Senators, the ultimate in official patrons. Like politicans today, they may not have known much about "art," but they surely knew what they liked. The message of Leutze's mural as directed by these patrons was, perhaps more than any other official work of art of the era, subject to continuous review and approval. Could any artist working under such scrutiny have struck a critical or discordant note?

The value of Weir's study is that through its sketchy, impromptu appearance the solidity and weight of the grand "official" mural, with its elaborate pretense of documenting America's westward migration, dissolves into the fugitive reality of a time and space bound process—a calculated manipulation of artistic imagination and technique. Weir's drawing provides a behind-the-scenes insight into the process of fabricating a major artifact of ideological consensus. Doubtless, a scene like that Weir captured could have been sketched for every image purporting to depict Daniel Boone; knowing that enables one to better grasp the methods of artifice and persuasion that such works represented for 19th-century Americans.

CHAPTER IX

Conclusion:
The Eclipse of Daniel Boone as a Visual Symbol

After the Civil War a new and more universal type of Western hero—the cowboy—became the focus of national fascination in the visual arts, and the figure of Daniel Boone all but disappeared. It seems surprising that no significant pictures of the pathfinder were painted by any major artists after Bingham's and Wimar's works of the early 1850s, although the production of books about Boone continued unabated. Bingham's frustration in securing a commission to paint Boone in the Capitol and Leutze's marginalization of the pioneer in his mural were symtomatic of this change. Clearly Daniel Boone's usefulness as a visual symbol of national expansion had been supplanted by new symbols more suited to the needs of an urban and industrial society.

The underlying reason for Daniel Boone's disappearance in the visual arts is that at the heart of the Boone legend there was a paradox. Depending on the artist and the audience in question, the Boone hero was expected to symbolize all things about the American experience of the frontier. He was to be a free-spirited hunter-wanderer or the upstanding bringer of civilization, the exemplar of white, Anglo-Saxon, Christian family values or a potential renegade white-Indian. He was ordained by Providence to accomplish his mission, but having served his purpose he was relegated to the margins as a venerated prophet of the new order, his place in the pantheon of art usurped by new, more universal masculine heroes like the cowboy.

Boone was a figure of history, and like any such figure he may have simply used up his effectiveness as a visual symbol. During the period of Boone's greatest activity the new country was only beginning to break out of the Appalachians, yet the two most important paintings of Boone were done when the nation was opening the trans-Mississippi West. In Leutze's painting Boone had become peripheral because of an expanded typological conception of westward emigration in which every settler could be a "type of young America" manifesting the progress of national destiny. By 1861, Boone's associations were too much those of the Revolutionary War era, and the opening of Kentucky seemed a moment in the distant past that paled in comparison with the Herculean effort required to conquer California and the Far West.

Endnotes

INTRODUCTION

1. For a comprehensive annotated bibliography of 19th-century sources on Boone see William Harvey Miner, *Daniel Boone: Contributions Toward a Bibliography of Writings Concerning Daniel Boone, 1901* (New York: Burt Franklin, 1970).

2. Only five works depicting Boone are listed in James L. Yarnell and William H. Gerdts, *The National Museum of American Arts Index to American Art Exhibition Catalogues From the Beginning through the 1876 Centennial Year* (Boston: G. K. Hall, 1986).

3. Hans-Georg Gadamer, *Philosophical Hermeneutics* (Berkeley, Calif.; University of California Press, 1976), 67. For a definition of hermeneuticism see Hans-Georg Gadamer, *Truth and Method*, trans. Sheed and Ward Ltd. (New York: Seabury Press, 1975); and the valuable collection of hermeneutic primary sources in *The Hermeneutics Reader*, ed. Kurt Mueller-Vollmer (New York: Continuum, 1989), also Jean Grondin, "Hermeneutics and Relativism," chap. in *Festivals of Interpretation*, ed. Kathleen Wright (Albany, N.Y.: State University of New York Press, 1990), 42-62.

4. Friedrich Nietzsche, *The Will to Power*, trans. Walter Kaufmann and R. J. Hollingdale (New York: Vintage, 1968), 267.

5. For a discussion of typology in the landscapes of Frederic Edwin Church see David C. Huntington, "Frederic Church's *Niagara*: Nature and the Nation's Type," *Texas Studies in Literature and Language* 25, no. 1 (Spring 1983): 100-138.

6. A valuable recent study of these tensions is Alexander Saxton, *The Rise and Fall of the White Republic: Class Politics and Mass Culture in Nineteenth-Century America* (New York: Verso, l990).

7. Sacvan Bercovitch, *The American Jeremiad* (Madison, Wisc.: University of Wisconsin Press, 1978), 164.

8. Frederick Jackson Turner, "The Significance of the Frontier in American History," *Proceedings of the Forty-First Meeting of the State Historical Society of Wisconsin* (Madison, Wisc.: 1894), 79-112, reprinted in Clyde A. Milner II, Ed., *Major Problems in the History of the American West* (Lexington, Mass.: D. C. Heath & Co., 1989), 7.

CHAPTER I

9. See Michael A. Lofaro, *The Life and Adventures of Daniel Boone* (Lexington, Ky.: University Press of Kentucky, 1986). See also the older but still useful biography of Boone by John Bakeless, *Daniel Boone: Master of the Wilderness*, 1939 (Harrisburg, Pa.,: Stackpole Co., 1965). Both Lofaro and Bakeless have based their studies on the Draper Manuscript Collection at the State Historical Society of Wisconsin. Dr. Lyman Copeland Draper, the 19th-century archivist and investigative historian spent fifty years gathering materials on Boone. The results fill 486 volumes, and he completed a five-volume manuscript "Life of Boone" that covers the Kentuckian's life to 1778, but remains unpublished.

10. Quoted in Lofaro, *Life and Adventures of Daniel Boone*, 5.

11. Ibid., 25.

12. See John Walton, "Ghost Writer to Daniel Boone," *American Heritage* 6, no. 6 (October 1955): 10-13. Also Walton's biography of Filson contains much useful information about Filson's land speculation, the production of his book, and its usefulness as promotion for land developers and settlers moving into Kentucky. See John Walton, *John Filson of Kentucke* (Lexington, Ky.: University of Kentucky Press, 1956).

13. See Bakeless, *Daniel Boone*, 87. There is evidence to suggest that this speech was transcribed fairly accurately by an eyewitness, although its rhetoric was evidently embellished by Anglo writers who recounted it.

14. Ibid., 87.

15. Quoted in Lofaro, *Life and Adventures of Daniel Boone*, 47.

16. John Filson, *The Discovery and Settlement of Kentucky... [and] The Adventures of Col. Daniel Boon* (Wilmington, Del.: John Adams, 1784; reprint, Ann Arbor, Mich.: University Microfilms, 1966), 60.

17. See Slotkin, *Regeneration Through Violence: The Mythology of the American Frontier, 1600-1860* (Middletown, Conn.: Wesleyan University Press, 1973), especially Chapter 13, "Man without a Cross: the Leatherstocking Myth," and also where Slotkin notes that "This incident was to be developed in elaborate detail by many later writers of the Romantic period—Cooper in *The Last of the Mohicans* and

other of the Leatherstocking tales, [Gilbert] Imlay in *The Emigrants*, and [Charles Brockden] Brown in *Edgar Huntly*...." 286. Slotkin observes that "The narratives relating to Boone's life—certainly the Filson text in Wilder's and Trumbull's editions and probably Flint's studies in the 1830s—formed part of [Cooper's] reading and supplied incidents and images to several novels in the cycle." 485.

18. Filson, *The Discovery and Settlement of Kentucke*, 65-66.
19. Lofaro, *The Life and Adventures of Daniel Boone*, 93.
20. Filson, *The Discovery and Settlement of Kentucke*, 77.
21. Quoted in Bakeless, *Daniel Boone*, 273-274. Girty's speech was first reported in John Bradford's rare periodical the *Kentucky Gazette* which was published from 1826-1829. It is presumably taken from the account of some white captive who heard it. See Bakeless note 455. The reference to rum makes it clear this speech reflects post-contact memories of European colonists.
22. James Fenimore Cooper, *The Prairie: A Tale*, 1827, ed. Henry Nash Smith (New York: Holt, Rinehart and Winston, 1950), 2.
23. Ibid., 3.
24. John James Audubon, *Delineations of American Scenery and Character*, ed. Francis Hobart Herrick (New York: G.A. Baker & Co., 1926), 60-61.
25. Bakeless, *Daniel Boone*, 413.
26. See Yarnell and Gerdts, *Index to American Art Exhibition Catalogues*, 2374.

CHAPTER II

27. Filson, *The Discovery and Settlement of Kentucke*, 5.
28. Ibid., 6.
29. Ibid., 81.
30. Ibid., 49-50.
31. Slotkin, *Regeneration Through Violence*, 272.
32. Filson, *The Discovery and Settlement of Kentucke*, 56.
33. Ibid., 81.
34. Just two years after Filson's book appeared, John Trumbull of Norwich, Connecticut, published the first of what would become a flood of pirated editions of Filson's text to appear over the next fifty years. Trumbull altered Filson's text by eliminating all of Boone's philosophical musings, emphasizing him as a man of decisive action. Gone are the Jeremiad-like passages of dark introspection replaced with an image of an Edenic Kentucky to which Trumbull uneasily joined another captivity narrative drawn from contemporary newspaper accounts. The popularity of Trumbull's text was attested to by its numerous reprintings, and by its incorporation into many later commentaries on the West well into the mid-19th century. See the facsimile of Trumbull's text in Willard Rouse Jillson, *The Boone Narrative* (Louisville, Ky.: Standard Printing Company, 1932). Jillson provided additional bibliographic citations of early Boone material supplementing Minor's 1901 compilation.
35. Chester Harding, *My Egotistigraphy* (Cambridge, Mass.: By John Wilson and Son, 1866), 35-36.
36. Ibid., 36.
37. Leah Lipton, "Chester Harding and the Life Portraits of Daniel Boone," *American Art Journal* 16, no. 3 (Summer 1984): 9.
38. See Leah Lipton, "George Caleb Bingham in the Studio of Chester Harding, Franklin, Mo., 1820," *American Art Journal* 16, no. 3 (Summer 1984): 90-92.
39. Lipton, "Chester Harding," 13.
40. The only substantial information of James Otto Lewis is found in Porter Butts, *Art in Wisconsin* (Madison, Wisc.: Democrat Publishing Co., 1936), 24-30. See also William H. Gerdt's *Art Across America*, (New York: Abbeville Press, 1990), Vol. 2, 231, 255, 329, for additional comments on Lewis's practice of art in Michigan and Wisconsin.
41. Cited in Lipton, "Chester Harding," 10.
42. Cited in Charles Van Ravenswaay, "A Rare Midwestern Print," *The Magazine Antiques* (February 1943): 77-78, and cited in Lipton, "Chester Harding," 10.
43. Dawn Glanz, *How the West Was Drawn: American Art and the Settling of the Frontier* (Ann Arbor, Mich.: UMI Research Press, 1982), 3.
44. Ibid., note 15.
45. Ibid., 4.
46. For a scholarly account of the role of guns in early American life see M. L. Brown, *Firearms in Colonial America: The Impact on History and Technology* (Washington, D.C.; Smithsonian Institution Press, 1980) and Louis A. Garavaglia and Charles G. Worman, *Firearms of the American West: 1803-1865* (Albuquerque, N.M.: University of New Mexico Press, 1984). An older, but still useful study is Charles Edward Chapel, *Guns of the Old West* (New York: Coward-McCann, 1961). For a perceptive popular account of the Kentucky long rifle see James E. Sterven, *Conquering the Frontiers* (La Habra, Calif.: Foundation Press, 1974), especially "The Long Rifles," 15-30.
47. For an extended study of the importance of dogs in frontier society see John E. Baur, *Dogs on the Frontier* (San Antonio, Texas: Naylor Company, 1964). For a scholarly accounting of the importance of dogs during an earlier period see John Grier Varner and Jeannette J. Varner, *Dogs of the Conquest* (Norman, Okla.: University of Oklahoma Press, 1983).
48. Cited in Lipton, "The Life Portraits of Daniel Boone," 13. From a transcription of the notice at the Filson Club, Louisville, Ky.

CHAPTER III

49. Daniel Bryan, *The Mountain Muse: Comprising the Adventures of Daniel Boone and the Powers of Virtuous and Refined Beauty* (Harrisonburg, Va.: Davidson & Bourne, 1813), 112.
50. Quoted in Lofaro, *The Life and Adventures of Daniel Boone*, 127.
51. C. Wilder, Ed. after John Filson, *Life and Adventures of Colonel Daniel Boone: The First White Settler of the State of Kentucky Written by Himself* (Brooklyn, N.Y.: By C. Wilder, 1823; reprint, Heartman's Historical Series no. 17, for Daniel Boone Club, n.d.).
52. Samuel Griswold Goodrich, Ed., *The Token, a Christmas and New Year's Present* (Boston, 1828), l:v. The painting was reproduced with a commentary by an unnamed author, perhaps Goodrich, entitled "The Solitary," with a lengthy two-page poem. The text for "The Solitary" offers a few passages that confirm the image of Boone as a loner.

"...[Boone's] principal food was obtained by hunting. An exploring traveler, sometimes crossing the way of this singular man, would find him seated at the door of his hut with his rifle across his knees, and his faithful dog at his side, surveying his shrivelled limbs, and lamenting that his youth and manhood were gone..." 48.

53. For a biographical study of Cole see Ellwood C. Parry, *The Art of Thomas Cole: Ambition and Imagination* (Newark, N.J.: University of Delaware Press, 1988). For a review of Parry's study see Alan Wallach, "Book Reviews," *Archives of American Art Journal* 28, no. 4 (1988): 21-25.

54. See Alan Wallach, "Thomas Cole and the Aristocracy," *Arts Magazine* 56 (November 1981): 94-106.

55. See Samuel Griswold Goodrich, *Recollections of a Lifetime: Or, Men and Things I Have Seen*, 2 vols. (New York: l857).

56. Wilder, *Life and Adventures of Colonel Daniel Boone*, 37. It is important to note that Wilder is actually commenting on a treatise by James Smith first published in 1812, but misattributed to Boone by Wilder.

57. For notes on this drawing and Cole's painting of Boone see Charles H. Morgan and Margaret C. Toole, "Notes on the Early Hudson River School," *Art in America* 39, no. 4 (December 1951): 161-177. Also Ellwood C. Parry, "Thomas Cole and the Problem of Figure Drawing," *American Art Journal* 4, no. 1 (Spring 1972): 66-86. Parry (p. 73) suggests that "It is much more likely, however, that this drawing was made in New York City where models were readily available and where Cole would have had access to a painted or published portrait of Daniel Boone." However, the only known portraits of Boone at this time were by Harding and the print by Lewis after Harding's portrait. The face of Cole's Boone bears no resemblance to that in Harding's painting or in the Lewis engraving, and it seems fair to suggest that it, like the rest of Cole's painting, was largely an invention.

58. Wilder, *Life and Adventures of Colonel Daniel Boone*, 30.

59. Ibid., 28.

60. Ibid., 33.

61. For Cole's early career see Louis Legrand Noble, *The Life and Works of Thomas Cole*, 1853, ed. Elliot S. Vesell (Cambridge, Mass.: Harvard University Press, 1964), especially chapters 3-5. Also Ellwood C. Parry, "Thomas Cole's Early Career: 1818-1829," chap. in *Views and Visions: American Landscape Before 1830* (Washington, D.C.: Corcoran Gallery of Art, 1986), 161-187.

62. Wilder, *Life and Adventures of Colonel Daniel Boone*, 29.

63. See Alan Wallach, "Cole, Byron and the *Course of Empire*," *Art Bulletin* 50 (December 1968): 375-379. Wallach notes, "Cole's interest in Byron may well have gone back to his youth in England." 377. In America, however, public admiration for Byron was inhibited by religious leaders and moralists who considered his character corrupt and his works immoral. For the American reaction to Byron see William Ellery Leonard, *Byron and Byronism in America*, 1905; reprint (New York 1965).

64. Wilder, *Life and Adventures of Colonel Daniel Boone*, 40.

65. Ibid., 29.

66. See J. Gray Sweeney, "The Nude of Landscape Painting: Emblematic Personification in the Hudson River School," *Smithsonian Studies in American Art* 3, no. 4 (Fall 1989): 47, for an extended discussion of anthropomorphic symbolism and its role in the expression of sentiment in the art of Cole and other American artists of the antebellum period.

CHAPTER IV

67. For a study of the Indian removal and its racist background see Reginald Horsman, *Race and Manifest Destiny: The Origins of American Racial Anglo-Saxonism* (Cambridge, Mass.: Harvard University Press, 1981).

68. Glanz, *How the West Was Drawn*, 14-15, 67-68 contains valuable discussions of Causici and Greenough's sculptures to which I am indebted.

69. Ibid., 14.

70. For a history of Greenough's work see Sylvia E. Crane, *White Silence: Greenough, Powers and Crawford, American Sculptors in Nineteenth Century Italy* (Coral Gables, Fla.: University of Miami Press, 1972). A more recent interpretive study is Vivien Fryd Green's "Two Sculptures for the Capitol: Horatio Greenough's *Rescue* and Luigi Persico's *Discovery of America*," *American Art Journal* 19, no. 2 (1987), 16-39.

71. Timothy Flint, *Biographical Memoir of Daniel Boone: The First Settler of Kentucky...* 1833, ed. James K. Folsom (New Haven, Conn.: College & University Press, 1967), 79.

72. Letter of 15 November 1837 to Secretary of State John Forsyth, quoted in Nathalia Wright, Ed., *Letters of Horatio Greenough: American Sculptor* (Madison, Wisc: University of Wisconsin Press, 1972), 221.

73. Letter of 14 March 1859 to Senator James Pearce, quoted in Crane, *White Silence*, 136.

74. Quoted in Wright, Ed., *Letters of Horatio Greenough*, 214.

75. Slotkin, *Regeneration Through Violence*, 440.

76. *Bulletin of the American Art-Union* (September 1851): 97.

77. *Family Magazine* (Cincinnati) 1, no. 3 (March 1836): 81.

78. Allan's portrait of Boone might have been included in the exhibition had not its condition, size and permanent installation in the Kentucky State Capitol prevented it being moved. See Roy T. King, "Portraits of Daniel Boone," *The Missouri Historical Review* 33, no. 2 (January 1939): 180.

79. It was described by Ruben Gold Thwaits in his 1902 biography of Boone as "an ideal sketch, of no special merit." Ruben Gold Thwaits, *Daniel Boone* (New York: D. Appleton & Co. 1902), note 238.

CHAPTER V

80. See William H. Gerdts and Mark Thistlethwaite, *Grand Illusions: History Painting in America* (Fort Worth, Texas: Amon Carter Museum, 1988), *passim*.

81. For a discussion of the evolution of history painting into genre painting see Thistlethwaite, "The Most Important Themes: History Painting and Its Place in American Art," chap. in *Grand Illusions: History Painting in America*, 7-58.

82. See William H. Truettner, "The Art of History: American Exploration and Discovery Scenes, 1840-1860." *American Art Journal* 14 (Winter 1982): 9, note 10. See also Truettner's expanded treatment of this theme in "Ideology and Image: Justifying Westward Expansion," chap. in *The West As America* (Washington, D.C.: Smithsonian

Institution Press, 1991), 27-53.

83. Cole's idea for the subject is listed as no. 118 in his list of potential paintings in the State Library of New York, Albany. See Howard Merritt, *Studies on Thomas Cole, An American Romanticist* (Baltimore, Md.: Baltimore Museum of Art, 1967), 99.

84. The most recent study of Ranney is Linda Ayres "William Ranney," chap. in *American Frontier Life: Early Western Paintings and Prints* (Fort Worth, Texas: Amon Carter Museum of Art, 1987), 79-107. Ayres does not discuss Ranney's paintings of Boone. Older, but still useful is Francis S. Grubar, *William Ranney: Painter of the Early West* (Washington, D.C.: Corcoran Gallery of Art, 1962).

85. Flint, *Biographical Memoir of Daniel Boone*, 23.

86. Ibid., 186-187.

87. Ibid., 186.

88. John M. Peck, *Life of Daniel Boone: Pioneer of Kentucky*, vol. 13, *The Library of American Biography*, ed. Jared Sparks (Boston, Mass.: Charles Little and James Brown, 1847), 5

89. Ibid., 8.

90. Ibid., 18.

91. Ibid., 150.

92. Ibid., 21.

93. Ibid., 196.

94. Slotkin, *Regeneration Through Violence*, 459.

95. Flint, *Biographical Memoir of Daniel Boone*, 51-55.

96. See Alan Wallach, "Making a Picture of the View from Mount Holyoke," *Bulletin of the Detroit Institute of Arts: The Drawings of Thomas Cole* 66, no. 1 (1990): 38.

97. Peck, *Life of Daniel Boone*, 23.

98. Ibid., 188.

99. "Movements of Artists," *The Literary World* no. 132 (11 August 1849): 113. I would like to thank Merl M. Moore, Jr. for bringing this notice to my attention.

100. Henry T. Tuckerman, "Over the Mountains, or The Western Pioneer," chap. in *The Home Book of the Picturesque* (New York: G.P. Putnam, 1852), 117.

101. Another reference to Boone as a type of Columbus occurs in William Gilmore Simms, "Daniel Boone: The First Hunter of Kentucky," published in Simms' *Southern and Western Magazine* 1 (April 1845): 225-242. In that essay the Southerner Simms depicts Boone as a courtier who would have been at ease with Simms' southern readers, but also as a figure who serves a national mission. "He was on a mission. The spiritual sense was strong in him. He felt the union between his inner self and the nature of the visible world, and yearned for their intimate communion. His thoughts and feelings were those of a great discoverer. He could realize the feelings of a Columbus or a Balboa, and thus gazing over the ocean waste of forest which then spread from the dim western outlines of the Alleghanies, to the distant and untravelled waters of the Mississippi, he was quite as much isolated as was ever any of the great admirals, who set forth, on the Atlantic, still dreaming of Cathay." 230.

102. Tuckerman, "Over the Mountains, or the Western Pioneer," 118.

103. For an account of Squire Boone see John Joseph Stoudt, "Daniel and Squire Boone—A Study in Historical Symbolism," *Pennsylvania History* 3, no. 1 (1936): 27-40.

104. Flint, *Biographical Memoir of Daniel Boone*, 61.

105. Peck, *Life of Daniel Boone*, 33.

106. "Fine Arts," *The Home Journal*, 30 April 1853, 2.

107. "The National Academy of Design," *New York Herald*, 23 May 1853, cited in Grabar, *William Ranney*, 41.

CHAPTER VI

108. Nancy Rash, *The Paintings and Politics of George Caleb Bingham* (New Haven, Conn.: Yale University Press, 1991),8.

109. See Lipton, "George Caleb Bingham," 90-91.

110. Cited in E. Maurice Bloch, *The Paintings of George C. Bingham: A Catalogue Raisonne* (Columbia, Mo.: University of Missouri Press, 1986), 131. See also E. Maurice Bloch, *George Caleb Bingham: The Evolution of an Artist* (Berkeley, Calif.: University of California Press, 1967), 123, note 149.

111. Bingham to James S. Rollins, Washington, 21 February 1841, quoted in C. B. Rollins, Ed., "Letters of George C. Bingham to James S. Rollins," *Missouri Historical Review* 23 (October 1937-July 1938), 10.

112. Rash, *The Paintings and Politics of George Caleb Bingham*, 20.

113. Bingham to James S. Rollins, Marshall, Mo., 2 November 1846, quoted in Rollins, "Letters of George C. Bingham to James S. Rollins," 16.

114. Ibid., 23 September 1844, Boonville, Mo., 13-14.

115. Ibid., 30 March, 1851, New York, 21. Bingham's claim that the subject of Daniel Boone was "one which has never yet been painted" is puzzling in light of the fact that Ranney's painting had been exhibited at the American Art-Union's annual exhibition in the Fall of 1850, and must have been on exhibition at the Art-Union gallery during the fall. Bingham arrived in New York by November 19, and would surely have seen Ranney's picture. Furthermore, the Art-Union *Bulletin* for May 1850 contained Alfred Jones's reproduction of Ranney's painting. In addition, as Bloch noted, it seems no coincidence that Bingham would also offer another picture in competition with Ranney when he created his Western sporting picture *Shooting for Beef*. Ranney had already achieved a considerable reputation with his Western pictures, and it is likely that Bingham was inspired to compete with him in the conception of his subjects. In any event Bingham's statement appears to be disingenuous, and may have been a crude attempt to manipulate his patrons at the Art-Union. See Bloch, *George Caleb Bingham*, 121, note 137.

116. "Fine Arts," *The Home Journal*, 12 April 1851, 3. I am grateful to Pamela Belanger for bringing this citation to my attention.

117. *Missouri Statesman*, 23 May 1851, 3, quoting the *St. Louis Republican*, 13 May 1851.

118. See Bloch, *The Paintings of George Caleb Bingham*, 195-196.

119. I am indebted to Duane Snedeker of the Missouri Historical Society, St. Louis for bringing this unusual image to my attention. The photograph will be published in a forthcoming book on the Society's collection of photographs.

120. I would like to thank the staff of the Conservation Laboratory of the St. Louis Art Museum for making available a video cassette recording of this scan of the

painting made on 7 June 1990, in conjunction with the Bingham exhibition at the Museum.

121. *Bulletin of the American Art-Union* (December 1851): 39.

122. Bloch is mistaken when he says in the 1967 edition of his book *George Caleb Bingham: The Evolution of An Artist*, 126-127, "The rather considerable repainting was confined mainly to the background, the *comparatively meaningless and topographically commonplace* selection of landscape elements being replaced by a forbidding aspect of high mountains and deep passes . . . ." (emphasis added) 126-127.

123. Bloch points out Rothermal's print as a possible source for the entire picture, but no figure with an ax is visible in the first version of the painting.

124. See my discussion of the symbolism of birds in Asher B. Durand's *Kindred Spirits*, in "Endued with Rare Genius: Frederic Edwin Church's *To the Memory of Cole*," *Smithsonian Studies in American Art* 2, no. 1 (Winter 1988): 64.

125. Filson, *The Discovery and Settlement of Kentucke*, 57-58.

126. See Richard W. Wallace, *Salvator Rosa in America*, (Wellesley, Mass.: Wellesley College Museum, 1979). See entry for "Bingham: *The Storm*," 123. Bingham's painting *The Storm*, circa 1850 (Wadsworth Atheneum, Hartford, Conn.) amply demonstrates the influence of Salvator Rosa on Bingham's art around 1850. A painting then thought to be one of the finest examples of Rosa's art in the United States was the work known as *Landscape with Mercury and Argus* at the Pennsylvania Academy of Fine Arts. Bingham could have seen the painting, which is now known to be by a follower of Rosa, during one of his stays in Philadelphia. Interestingly, this work also influenced the direction of Thomas Cole's art when he worked in the city.

127. See Sweeney, "The Nude of Landscape Painting," *passim*.

128. Although Bloch does not indicate any specific examples, he notes in *Evolution of an Artist* that "It can be assumed that Bingham had come into contact with the works of Thomas Cole as early as 1838, when he could have seen his pictures on exhibition at the National Academy of Design.... The dynamic, grandiose tendency of Cole ... could not have failed to attract his attention. That awareness is best demonstrated in a landscape like *The Storm*.... One is strongly reminded of Cole's own representations of a dynamic and untamed nature, and even the blasted tree motif used so frequently by Bingham in his pictures, can be ultimately traced to Cole." 128.

129. See Sweeney, "Endued with Rare Genius," 45-72, for a discussion of these memorials and their influence, especially note 20.

130. Cited in Bloch, *The Paintings of George Caleb Bingham*, 19, note 68. Bloch asserted that Bingham may have actually provided this reference to the editor of the *Statesman*, his close friend William F. Switzler. The notion that it was the *exclusive* source seems to deny the artist's eclecticism in relying on multiple sources for his imagery as to be untenable. Dawn Glanz was the first to point out the importance of Peck for the development of Bingham's imagery.

131. Peck, *Life of Daniel Boone*, 23-24.

132. Ibid., 39.

133. Elizabeth Johns is the first modern scholar to clearly call attention to the class consciousness that pervades the figures in this and other paintings by Bingham. See her important essay "The 'Missouri Artist' as Artist," chap. in Michael E. Shapiro, Ed., *George Caleb Bingham* (St. Louis, Mo.: St. Louis Art Museum, and New York: Harry N. Abrams, 1990), 133-139.

134. Bingham to Sarah Elizabeth Hutchison, Columbia, Mo., 16 February 1835, quoted in Bloch, *The Paintings of George Caleb Bingham*, 4.

135. Bingham to James S. Rollins, 21 February 1841, Washington, D.C., quoted in C. B. Rollins, "Letters of George C. Bingham," 12.

136. In a passage attached to the painting of *Prometheus Bound* (Collection Philadelphia Museum of Art & Catskill Public Library) Cole wrote of the classical god, "Prometheus is left attached to the mountain in the manner of one crucified." Cited in Parry, *The Art of Thomas Cole*, Plate 18.

137. Bloch, *Evolution of an Artist*, 128.

138. For a study of the Republican symbolism of Cincinnatus see Garry Wills, *Cincinnatus: George Washington and the Enlightenment* (Garden City, N.J.: Doubleday, 1984).

139. These symbolic associations have been noted by many modern scholars. The first to observe it was Patricia Hills in *The American Frontier: Images and Myths* (New York: Whitney Museum of American Art, 1973), 8. Maurice Bloch does not mention the idea in either of his two studies on Bingham.

140. See Rash's extended discussion of this issue in chap. 4 "From Snags to Slavery" in *The Painting and Politics of George Caleb Bingham*, 94-119. Rash thoroughly discusses Bingham's intense preoccupation with the issue of slavery.

141. Bingham to James S. Rollins, Independence, Mo., 21 June 1855, quoted in C. B. Rollins, "Letters of George C. Bingham," 189.

142. See Paul C. Nagel, "The Man and His Times," chap. in Shapiro, *George Caleb Bingham*, 40-41. Nagel reports, "Chattel bondage had no enemy in Bingham. In 1850, George [Bingham] owned a male and a female slave. Three years later he took four more slaves from his sister Amanda when he bought her share of Mary Bingham's estate.... The much-admired James Rollins claimed to have twenty-four [slaves]."

143. In a letter to John S. Rollins written on 2 June 1856, from Louisville, Ky., Bingham wrote, "These reports [from the western frontier] convince me more strongly than ever that Slavery is doomed, and that Providence is determined to use its brutalized champions at the instruments of its overthrow." The letter is useful as yet another affirmation of Bingham's adamant antislavery position, but also as an example of how the common idea that national affairs, particularly the elimination of the social and political injustice of slavery, would be determined by "Providence." Quoted in C. B. Rollins, "Letters of George C. Bingham," 195.

144. For a useful study of the shifting nature of Whig ideology see Thomas Brown, *Politics and Statesmanship: Essays on the*

American Whig Party (New York: Columbia University Press, 1985)

145. Glanz, *How the West Was Drawn*, 23.

146. Bingham to James S. Rollins, Philadelphia, 12 December 1853, quoted in C. B. Rollins, "Letters of George C. Bingham," 172.

147. Ibid., Philadelphia, 12 January 1855, 187.

148. Ibid., Düsseldorf, West Germany, 3 June 1857, 353.

149. Ibid., Düsseldorf, West Germany, 12 October 1857, 357.

150. Ibid., Düsseldorf, West Germany, 18 July 1858, 364.

151. Ibid., 356.

152. Ibid., 365.

153. Ibid., 365-366.

CHAPTER VII

154. See Benjamin Poff Draper, "American Indians—Barbizon Style," *Antiques* 44 (September 1943): 108-110, and "From Fontainebleau to the Dark and Bloody Ground," *Month at Goodspeed's Book Shop* (Boston), 16 (March-April 1945): 150-154.

155. Peck, *Life of Daniel Boone*, 58-59.

156. See De Cost Smith, "Jean François Millet's Drawing of American Indians," *The Century Illustrated Monthly Magazine* 80, new series Vol. 58 (May-October 1910): 79-85.

157. Peck, *Life of Daniel Boone*, 59-60.

158. I am grateful to Joseph D. Ketner for sharing his insights on Wimar with me for this chapter. All references and excerpts from his study are used with his permission. See Ketner, "The Indian Painter in Düsseldorf," chpt. in *Carl Wimar: Chronicler of the Missouri River Frontier* (Fort Worth, Tx.: Amon Carter Museum, 1991).

159. Quoted in Ketner, "Indian Painter in Düsseldorf," 44.

160. Peck, *The Life of Daniel Boone*, 61-62.

161. See "$19,365 Burglary at the Home of Louis S. Denning" *St. Louis Post Dispatch*, 1 November 1949. The article noted that "The two paintings stolen were by the late Carl Wimar, noted painter of western subjects. One 'Discovery of Daniel Boone's camp,' is valued at $2500."

162. Ketner, "Indian Painter in Düsseldorf," 49.

163. See Joseph D. Ketner, "Abduction, Rape and Redemption on the Frontier: Carl Wimar's *Abduction of Daniel Boone's Daughter by the Indians*," unpublished manuscript. I am grateful to Ketner for sharing this study with me in a draft form.

164. I am indebted to Joseph D. Ketner for sharing his ideas about this painting text in his original, unedited manuscript form with me.

165. See Phillips D. Carleton, "The Indian Captivity," *American Literature* 19 (March 1947): 1-20, cited in Ketner, 54.

166. Cecil B. Hartley, *Life of Daniel Boone, the Great Western Hunter and Pioneer...* (New York: Lovell, Coryell & Company, 1859), n.p.

CHAPTER VIII

167. One of the earliest expression of the creed was Timothy Dwight's celebration of westward expansion in his poem *Greenfield Hill*.

> All hail, thou western world! by heaven design'd
> Th' example bright, to renovate mankind.
> Soon shall thy sons across the mainland roam;
> And claim, on far Pacific shores, their home;
> Their rule, religion, manners arts convey . . . .

Timothy Dwight, *Greenfield Hill* (New York: Childs and Swaine, 1794), 52 reprinted ed. in William J. McTaggard and William K. Bottorff, Eds., *The Major Poems of Timothy Dwight* (Gainesville, Fla.: Scholars' Facsimiles & Reprints, 1969), 418.

168. John L. O'Sullivan, "The True Title," *New York Morning News*, 27 December 1845, n.p.

169. Philip Schaff, *America: A Sketch of Its Political, Social, and Religious Character*, ed. Perry Miller (Cambridge, Mass.: Harvard University Press, 1961), quoted in Bercovitch, *The American Jeremiad*, 168.

170. C. W. Dana, *The Garden of the World, or the Great West: Its History, Its Wealth, Its Natural Advantages, and Its Future* (Boston: Wentworth, 1856), 13.

171. For a useful study of Gilpin see Thomas L. Karnes, *William Gilpin: Western Nationalist* (Austin, Texas: University of Texas Press, 1970).

172. William Gilpin, *The Mission of the North American People: Geographical, Social, and Political*, 2d ed. (Philadelphia, Pa.: J. B. Lippincott, 1873), 124. First published in 1860 as *The Central Gold Region*.

173. Ibid., 91 (Italics in original).

174. Ibid., 99.

175. Ibid., 8.

176. For a useful study of Crofutt and the painting he commissioned from Gast, indeed that he dictated to Gast, see Valerie J. Fifer, *American Progress: The Growth of the Transport, Tourist and Information Industries in the Nineteenth-Century West, Seen through the Life and Times of George A. Crofutt, Pioneer and Publicist of the Transcontinental Age* (Chester, Conn.: Globe Pequot, 1988).

177. George A. Crofutt, *Crofutt's New Overland Tourist and Pacific Coast Guide* (Chicago: Overland, 1878), n.p.

178. "Search Begun for Unusual Flag Presented to Lincoln in 1861," *Chicago Sun*, 11 February 1947, n.p. According to Herbert Levy, Archivists of K.A.M. Temple Isaiah Israel, Chicago, more than four decades of searching by members of the Temple have failed to uncover the location of the flag. The Temple preserves the circa 1861 glass plate photographic negative showing the banner. I am indebted to Mr. Herbert Levy of K.A.M. Temple for providing a photograph of Kohn's flag and generously allowing it to be reproduced here.

179. See Sacvan Bercovitch, *The Puritan Origins of the American Self* (New Haven, Conn.: Yale University Press, 1975) and *The American Jeremiad*; Ursula Brumm, *American Thought and Religious Typology* (New Brunswick, N.J.; Rutgers University Press, 1970); Perry Miller, *The New England Mind: The Seventeenth Century* (Cambridge, Mass.: Harvard University Press, 1939) reissued 1954 as *The New England Mind: From Colony to Province* (Cambridge, Mass.: Harvard University Press); also Perry Miller, *Errand into the Wilderness* (Cambridge, Mass.: Harvard University Press, 1954).

180. *Daily Illinois State Journal* (Springfield), 7 February 1861, 3:7. I am grateful to Merl M. Moore, Jr. for bringing this unusual review of Kohn's flag to my attention. It is more than coincidence that at about the same time the painter George Caleb Bingham was installing portraits of Henry Clay and Andrew Jackson in the Capitol Building in Jefferson City, Mo., and when called upon by the grateful politicians to make a speech he "made the Union and the Star Spangled Banner" his theme. Such was the patriotic fervor on the eve of Lincoln's inauguration against the backdrop of an impending Civil War. Bingham's comments are cited in a letter to James S. Rollins, Jefferson City, 12 January 1861, quoted in C. B. Rollins, "Letters of George C. Bingham," 505.

181. For Leutze's biography and career see Barbara S. Groseclose, *Emanuel Leutze, 1816-1868: Freedom Is the Only King* (Washington, DC: Smithsonian Institution Press, 1975), 60-62, 96-97.

182. *Boston Transcript*, 8 December 1862, 4. I would like to thank Merl M. Moore for sharing this review with me.

183. "Literature and Art: Leutze at Washington," *The Home Journal*, 6 July 1861, 2.

184. "Leutze's New Picture at the Capitol: Emigration to the West," *The [New York] Evening Post*, 17 December, 1862, 1.

185. Tuckerman, *Book of the Artists*, 336. Tuckerman noted that the mural "celebrates a primary cause of our national growth—Western Emigration." The commentary in Tuckerman's book first appeared in *The [New York] Evening Post*, 17 December 1862, 1.

186. *Boston Transcript*, 8 December 1862, 4.

187. Ibid.

188. Ibid.

189. "Leutze's New Picture at the Capitol," 1.

190. For a different view of Leutze's pictures see Glanz, *How the West Was Drawn*, 80. Glanz sees the work in relationship to the "millenniast spirit" of the abolitionists in the Civil War period. Millennialism was yet another aspect of the larger framework of typology with its encompassing vision of an unfolding divine plan of history. Glanz astutely observes that "[Leutze's] vision of westward emigration presents the West as the locality in which the millennial Golden Age was to be instituted in the aftermath of the [Civil] War."

191. For a useful history of the mural commission and its execution see Raymond Louis Stehle, "'Westward Ho!': The History of Leutze's Fresco in the Capitol," *Records of the Columbia Historical Society of Washington, D.C. 1960-1962* (Washington, D.C.: 1963), 306-322. For additional documentation on the commission see Charles E. Fairman, *Art and Artists of the Capitol of the United States of America* (Washington, D.C.: U.S. Government Printing Office, Vol. 95, 1927), 201-204.

192. Quoted in Fairman, *Art and Artists of the Capitol*, 202.

193. See Patricia Hills, "Picturing Progress in the Era of Westward Expansion," chap. in William Truettner, *The West As America*, 119.

194. Cited in Justin G. Turner, "Westward the Course of Empire Takes its Way," *Manuscripts* 18, no. 2 (September 1966): 15.

195. Nathaniel Hawthorne, "Chiefly about War Matters," *Atlantic Monthly* 10 (July 1862): 46.

196. Anne Brewster, "Emanuel Leutze: The Artist," *Lippincott's Magazine* 2 (November 1868): 536.

197. Cited in Turner, "Westward the Course of Empire," 11.

198. See Truettner, "Prelude to Expansion: History as Theater," chap. in *The West As America*, 64-65. I would like to thank Arthur J. Phelan for sharing additional information about this work with me.

Selected Bibliography

Primary Sources

Abbott, John S. C. *Daniel Boone, Pioneer of Kentucky*. New York, 1872.

Bogart, William H. *Daniel Boone and the Hunters of Kentucky*. New York, 1857.

Boston Transcript, 8 December 1862, 4.

Brewster, Anne. "Emanuel Leutze: The Artist." *Lippincott's Magazine* 2 (November 1868): 536.

Bryan, Daniel. *The Mountain Muse: Comprising the Adventures of Daniel Boone and the Powers of Virtuous and Refined Beauty*. Harrisonburg, Va: Davidson and Bourne, 1813.

Bulletin of the American Art-Union, (September 1851): 97.

Bulletin of the American Art-Union, (December 1851): 39.

Butler, Mann. *A History of the Commonwealth of Kentucky*. Louisville: Wilcox, Dickerman, 1834.

Church, [Benjamin and] Thomas. *The History of King Philip's War, Commonly Called the Great Indian War, of 1675 and 1676....* Edited by Samuel G. Drake. Exeter, N.H.: J. and B. Williams, 1829.

Cooper, James Fenimore. *The Prairie: A Tale*. Edited by Henry Nash Smith. New York: Holt, Rinehart and Winston, 1950.

Crofutt, George A. *Crofutt's New Overland Tourist and Pacific Coast Guide*. Chicago: Overland, 1878.

Daily Illinois State Journal (Springfield), 7 February 1861, 3:7.

Dana, C. W. *The Garden of the World, or the Great West: Its History, Its Wealth, Its Natural Advantages, and Its Future*. Boston: Wentworth, 1856.

Durrett, Reuben T. *Bryant's Station*. Louisville, Ky., 1897.

Dwight, Timothy. *Greenfield Hill: A Poem in Seven Parts*. New York: Childs and Swaine, 1794.

Family Magazine (Cincinnati) 1, no. 3 (March 1836): 81.

Filson, John. *The Discovery and Settlement of Kentucke... [and] The Adventures of Col. Daniel Boon*. Wilmington, Del.: John Adams, 1784; reprint, Ann Arbor, Mich.: University Microfilms, 1966.

_____. *The Adventures of Colonel Daniel Boon. One of the First Settlers at Kentucke....* Norwich: John Trumbull, 1786.

"Fine Arts." *The Home Journal*, 12 April 1851, 3.

"Fine Arts." *The Home Journal*, 30 April 1853, 2.

Flint, Timothy. *Indian Wars of the West*. Cincinnati, Ohio: 1833.

_____. *Biographical Memoir of Daniel Boone: The First Settler of Kentucky....* Reprinted from the Cincinnati, 1833 edition. Edited by James K. Folsom. New Haven, Conn.: College and University Press, 1967.

French, Benjamin Franklin. *Biographia Americana; or a Historical and Critical Account of the Lives, Actions, and Writings of the Most Distinguished Persons in North America....* New York: 1825.

Gilpin, William. *Mission of the North American People, Geographical, Social, and Political*. Philadelphia: J.B. Lippincott & Co., 1873.

Goodrich, Samuel Griswold. *Recollections of a Lifetime: Or, Men and Things I Have Seen*. 2 vols. New York: 1857.

_____, Ed. *The Token, A Christmas and New Year's Present*. Boston: 1828.

Hall, James. *Legends of the West*. Philadelphia: 1832.

Harding, Chester. *My Egotistigraphy*. Cambridge, Mass.: By John Wilson and Son, 1866.

_____. *A Sketch of Chester Harding: Artist, Drawn by His Own Hand*. Edited by Margaret E. White. 1890; reprint, New York: 1929; reprint of 1929 edition, New York: 1970.

Hawthorne, Nathaniel. "Chiefly About War Matters." *Atlantic Monthly* 10 (July 1862): 46.

Home Journal, 12 April 1851, 3.

Imlay, Gilbert. *A Topographical Description of the Western Territory of North America....* New York: 1793.

Irving, Washington. *Astoria: Or, Anecdotes of an Enterprise Beyond the Rocky Mountains*. Vol. 2. New York: Thomas Y. Crowell, n.d.

Jackson, Helen Hunt. *A Century of Dishonor: A Sketch of the United States Government's Dealings with Some of the Indian Tribes*. New York: Harper and Brothers, 1881.

"Leutze's New Picture at the Capitol: Emigration to the West." *The [New York] Evening Post*, 17 December 1862, 1.

"Literature and Art: Leutze at Washington." *The Home Journal*, 6 July 1861, 2.

Longacre, James B. *National Portrait Gallery of Distinguished Americans*. Philadelphia: Henry Perkins, 1835.

_____. *National Portrait Gallery of Eminent Americans*. Vol. 2. New York: 1861.

McClung, John A. *Sketches of Western Adventure: Containing an Account of the Most Interesting Incidents Connected with the Settlement of the West*. Louisville, Ky.: Richard H. Collins, 1879.

Marshall, Humphrey. *The History of Kentucky*. Frankfort, Ky.: Humphrey Marshall, 1812.

Metcalf, Samuel L. *A Collection of Some of the Most Interesting Narratives of Indian Warfare in the West*. Lexington, Ky., 1821.

Missouri Statesman, 23 May 1851, 3.

"Movements of Artists." *The Literary World*, no. 132 (11 August 1849): 113.

Noble, Louis Legrand. *The Life and Works of Thomas Cole*. 1853. Edited by Elliot S. Vesell. Cambridge: Harvard University Press, 1964.

O'Sullivan, John L. "The True Title." *New York Morning News*, 27 December 1845.

Peck, John M. *The Life of Daniel Boone: Pioneer of Kentucky*. Vol. 13, *The Library of American Biography*. Edited by Jared Sparks. Boston: Charles C. Little and James Brown, 1847.

Pritts, Joseph. *Incidents of Border Life, Illustrative of the Times and Conditions of the First Settlements in Parts of the Middle and Western States....* Chambersburg, Pa.: Joseph Pritts, 1839.

Rollins, C.B., Ed. "Letters of George Caleb Bingham to James S. Rollins." *Missouri Historical Review* 32, (October 1937-January 1938), *passim*.

"Search Begun for Unusual Flag Presented to Lincoln in 1861." *Chicago Sun*, 11 February 1947.

Simms, William Gilmore. "Daniel Boone—The First Hunter of Kentucky." *Southern and Western Magazine* 1 (April 1845): 225-242.

Triplett, Frank. *Conquering the Wilderness*. Minneapolis: Northwestern Publishing Co., 1888.

Tuckerman, Henry T. *Book of the Artists: American Artists Life*. New York: G. P. Putnam & Sons, 1967.

_____. "Over the Mountains, or The Western Pioneer." Chap. in *The Home Book of the Picturesque*. New York: G. P. Putnam, 1852.

Turner, Frederick Jackson. "The Significance of the Frontier in American History." *Proceedings of the Forty-First Meeting of the State Historical Society of Wisconsin*. Madison, Wisc.: 1894, 79-112.

Wilder, C., Ed. [after] John Filson. *Life and Adventures of Colonel Daniel Boone: The First White Settler of the State of Kentucky Written by Himself*. Brooklyn, N.Y.: By C. Wilder, 1823; reprint, Heartman Historical Series, no. 17, for Daniel Boone Club, n.d.

Secondary Sources

"$19,365 Burglary at the Home of Louis S. Denning." *St. Louis Post Dispatch*, 1 November 1949.

Adams, Henry. "A New Interpretation of Bingham's *Fur Traders Descending the Missouri*." *Art Bulletin* 65 (1983): 675-680.

_____. "Bingham and His Sources." *Art Bulletin* 66 (1984): 515.

Alvord, Clarence W. "Daniel Boone." *American Mercury* 8 (June 1926): 266-270.

Athearn, Robert G. *The Mythic West*. Lawrence, Kan.: University of Kansas Press, 1989.

Audubon, John James. *Delineations of American Scenery and Character*. Edited by Francis Hobart Herrick. New York: G. A. Baker & Co., 1926.

Ayres, Linda. "William Ranney." Chap. in *American Frontier Life: Early Western Paintings and Prints*. Fort Worth, Texas: Amon Carter Museum of Art, 1987.

Bakeless, John. *Daniel Boone: Master of the Wilderness*. 1939. Harrisburg, Pa.: Stackpole Co., 1965.

Barrell, John. *The Dark Side of the Landscape: The Rural Poor in English Painting 1730-1840*. Cambridge, England: Cambridge University Press, 1980.

Baur, John E. *Dogs on the Frontier*. San Antonio, Texas: Naylor Company, 1964.

Baxandall, Michael. *Patterns of Intention: On the Historical Explanation of Pictures*. New Haven, Conn.: Yale University Press, 1989.

Behrendt, Stephen C. "Originality and Influence in George Caleb Bingham's Art." *Great Plains Quarterly* 5 (1985): 24-38.

Bercovitch, Sacvan. "The Image of America: From Hermeneutics to Symbolism." *Bucknell Review* 20, no. 2 (Fall 1972): 3-12.

_____. *The Puritan Origins of the American Self*. New Haven, Conn.: Yale University Press, 1975.

_____. *The American Jeremiad*. Madison, Wisc.: University of Wisconsin Press, 1978.

Bercovitch, Sacvan, and Myra Jehlen. *Ideology and Classic American Literature*. Cambridge, Mass.: Harvard University Press, 1987.

Berkhofer, Robert F. *The White Man's Indian*. New York: Alfred Knopf, 1978.

Bermingham, Ann. *Landscape and Ideology: The English Rustic Tradition, 1740-1860*. Berkeley, Calif.: University of California Press, 1986.

Billington, Ray Allen. *Westward Expansion: A History of the American Frontier*. 1949, 1967, 1974. New York: 1982.

Bloch, E. Maurice. "Art in Politics." *Art in America* 33 (1945): 93-100.

_____. *George Caleb Bingham: The Evolution of an Artist*. Berkeley, Calif.: University of California Press, 1967.

_____. *The Drawings of George Caleb Bingham*. Columbia, Mo.: University of Missouri Press, 1975.

_____. *The Paintings of George Caleb Bingham: A Catalogue Raisonne*. Columbia, Mo.: University of Missouri Press, 1986.

Brown, Glenn. *History of the United State Capitol*. 1900; reprint, New York: Da Capo, 1970.

Brown, M. L. *Firearms in Colonial America: The Impact on History and Technology*. Washington, D.C.: Smithsonian Institution Press, 1980.

Brown, Thomas. *Politics and Statesmanship: Essays on the American Whig Party*. New York: Columbia University Press, 1985.

Bruce, Chris, Brian W. Dippie, and others. *Myth of the West*. Seattle, Wash.: Henry Art Gallery, 1990.

Bruce, Henry Addington. *Daniel Boone and the Wilderness Road*. New York: 1910.

Brumm, Ursula. *American Thought and Religious Typology*. New Brunswick, N.J.: Rutgers University Press, 1970.

Bryant, Keith. "George Caleb Bingham: The Artist as a Whig Politician," *Missouri Historical Review* 59 (1964-65): 448-463.

Butts, Porter. *Art in Wisconsin*. Madison, Wisc.: Democrat Publishing Co., 1936.

Byron, George Gordon, Lord. *Byron's Don Juan: A Variorum Edition*. Edited by Truman Guy Steffan and Willis W. Pratt. 4 vols. Austin, Texas: University of Texas Press, 1957.

Campbell, Joseph. *The Hero with a Thousand Faces*. New York: World, Meridian Books, 1949.

Carleton, Phillips D. "The Indian Captivity." *American Literature* 19 (March 1943): 1-20.

Chambers, William N. *Old Bullion Benton: Senator from the New West*. Boston: Little, Brown, 1956.

Chapel, Charles Edward. *Guns of the Old West*. New York:

Coward-McCann, 1961.

Christ-Janer, Albert. *George Caleb Bingham: Frontier Painter of Missouri.* New York: Abrams, 1975.

Collins, Charles D. "A Source for Bingham's Fur Traders Descending the Missouri." *Art Bulletin* 66 (1984): 678-681.

Cooper, James Fenimore. *The Deerslayer: Or, The First Warpath.* New York: Harper and Brothers, 1926.

Crane, Sylvia E. *White Silence: Greenough, Powers and Crawford, American Sculptors in Nineteenth Century Italy.* Coral Gables, Fla.: University of Miami Press, 1972.

Crevecoeur, Michel Guillaume St. Jean De. *Letters from an American Farmer.* Edited by Warren Barton Blake. New York: E. P. Dutton, 1957.

Cronon, William. "Revisiting the Vanishing Frontier." *Western Historical Quarterly* 18 (April 1987): 157-176.

Demos, John. "George Caleb Bingham: The Artist as Social Historian." *American Quarterly* 17 (1965): 218-228.

Draper, Benjamin Poff. "American Indians—Barbizon Style." *Antiques* 44 (September 1943): 108-110.

Drinnon, Richard. *Facing West: The Metaphysics of Indian Hating and Empire Building.* Minneapolis: University of Minnesota Press, 1980.

Ekirch, Arthur Alphonse, Jr. *The Idea of Progress in America, 1815-1860.* 1944, 1951. New York: AMS Press, 1969.

Ewers, John. *Artists of the Old West.* 1965, 1973. Garden City, N.Y.: Doubleday, 1982.

Fairman, Charles E. *Art and Artists of the Capitol of the United States of America.* Washington, D.C.: Government Printing Office, 1927.

Fifer, J. Valerie. *American Progress: The Growth of the Transport, Tourist, and Information Industries in the Nineteenth-Century West....* Chester, Conn.: Globe Pequot, 1988.

Ford, Alice, Ed. *Audubon by Himself.* Garden City, N.Y.: Natural History Press, 1968.

"From Fontainebleau to the Dark and Bloody Ground." *Month at Goodspeed's Book Shop* (Boston), 16 (March-April 1945): 150-154.

Gadamer, Hans-Georg. *Truth and Method.* Translated by Sheed and Ward Ltd. New York: Seabury Press, 1975.

Garavaglia, Louis A., and Charles G. Worman. *Firearms of the American West: 1803-1865.* Albuquerque, N.M.: University of New Mexico Press, 1984.

Gerdts, William H. *Art Across America,* 3 Vols. New York: Abbeville Press, 1990.

Gerdts, William H., and Mark Thistlethwait. *Grand Illusions: History Painting in America.* Fort Worth, Texas: Amon Carter Museum, 1988.

Glanz, Dawn. *How the West Was Drawn: American Art and the Settling of the Frontier.* Ann Arbor, Mich.: UMI Research Press, 1982.

Glassie, Henry. "Meaningful Things and Appropriate Myths: The Artifacts Place in American Studies." *Prospects* 3 (1977): 1-49.

Goetzmann, William H. *Exploration and Empire: The Explorer and the Scientist in the Winning of the American West.* New York: Knopf, 1966.

_____. *The West of the Imagination.* New York: W.W. Norton, 1986.

Green, Vivien Fryd. "Two Sculptures for the Capitol: Horatio Greenough's Rescue and Luigi Persico's Discovery of America."

American Art Journal 19, no. 2 (1987): 16-39.

Groseclose, Barbara S. *Emanuel Leutze, 1816-1868: Freedom Is the Only King.* Washington, D.C.: Smithsonian Institution Press, 1975.

_____. "Painting, Politics and George Caleb Bingham." *American Art Journal* 10 (1978): 5-19.

_____. "Politics and American Genre Painting of the Nineteenth Century." *Antiques* 120 (1981): 1210-1217.

Grubar, Francis S. *William Ranney: Painter of the Early West.* Washington, D.C.: Corcoran Gallery of Art, 1962.

Hadlin, Oscar. *Race and Nationality in American Life.* Garden City, N.Y.: Doubleday, Anchor Books, 1957.

Hassrick, Peter H. *The Way West: Art of Frontier America.* New York: Abrams, 1977.

Hills, Patricia. *The American Frontier: Images and Myths.* New York: Whitney Museum of American Art, 1973.

Honor, Hugh. *The New Golden Land: European Images of America from the Discoveries to the Present Time.* New York: Pantheon Books, 1975.

Horsman, Reginald. *Race and Manifest Destiny: The Origins of American Racial Anglo-Saxonism.* Cambridge, Mass.: Harvard University Press, 1981.

Howe, Daniel W. *The Political Culture of the American Whigs.* Chicago: University of Chicago Press, 1979.

Huntington, David C. *The Landscapes of Frederic Edwin Church: Vision of an American Era.* New York: George Braziller, 1966.

_____. "Frederic Church's *Niagara:* Nature and the Nation's Type." *Texas Studies in Literature and Language* 25, no. 1 (Spring 1983), 100-138.

Husch, Gail E. "George Caleb Bingham's *The County Election:* Whig Tribute to the Will of the People." *American Art Journal* 19, no. 4 (1987): 5-22.

Jillson, Willard Rouse. *Filson's Kentucky.* Louisville, Ky.: 1930.

_____. *Tales of the Dark and Bloody Ground.* Louisville, Ky.: 1930.

_____. *The Boone Narrative.* Louisville, Ky.: Standard Printing Company, 1932.

Karnes, Thomas L. *William Gilpin: Western Nationalist.* Austin, Texas: University of Texas Press, 1970.

Kasson, John F. *Civilizing the Machine: Technology and Republican Values in America, 1776-1900.* New York: Grossman, 1976.

Kenton, Edna. *Simon Kenton: His Life and Period, 1755-1836.* Garden City, N.Y.: 1930.

King, Roy T. "Portraits of Daniel Boone." *The Missouri Historical Review* 33, no. 2 (January 1939): 171-183.

Landow, George P. *Victorian Types Victorian Shadows: Biblical Typology in Victorian Literature, Art, and Thought.* Boston: Routledge & Kegan Paul, 1980.

Lears, T. J. Jackson. *No Place of Grace: Antimodernism and the Transformation of American Culture.* New York: Pantheon, 1981.

Leonard, William Ellery. *Byron and Byronism in America.* 1905; reprint, New York: 1965.

Lewis, R. W. B. *The American Adam.* Chicago: University of Chicago Press, 1955.

Limerick, Patricia Nelson. *The Legacy of Conquest: The Unbroken Past of the American West.* New York: W. W. Norton & Co., 1988.

Lipton, Leah. "Chester Harding and the Life Portraits of Daniel

Boone." *American Art Journal* 16, no. 3 (Summer 1984): 4-19.

_____. "George Caleb Bingham in the Studio of Chester Harding, Franklin, Mo., 1820." *American Art Journal* 16, no. 3 (Summer 1984): 90-92.

_____. *A Truthful Likeness: Chester Harding and His Portraits.* Washington, D.C.: National Portrait Gallery, 1985.

Lofaro, Michael A. "The Eighteenth Century 'Autobiographies' of Daniel Boone." *The Register of Kentucky Historical Society* 76 (1978): 85-97.

_____. "From Boone to Crockett: The Beginnings of Frontier Humor." *Mississippi Folklore Register* 14 (1980): 57-74.

_____. "Tracking Daniel Boone: The Changing Frontier in American Life." *The Register of the Kentucky Historical Society* 82 (1984): 321-333.

_____. *The Life and Adventures of Daniel Boone.* Lexington, Ky.: University Press of Kentucky, 1986.

_____. *The Tall Tales of Davy Crockett: The Second Nashville Series of Crockett Almanacs 1839-1841.* Knoxville, Tenn.: University of Tennessee Press, 1987.

Lowenthal, David. *The Past is a Foreign Country.* Cambridge: Cambridge University Press, 1985.

McDermott, John F. *George Caleb Bingham: River Portraitist.* Norman, Okla.: University of Oklahoma Press, 1959.

McTaggard, William J., and William K. Bottorff, Eds. *The Major Poems of Timothy Dwight.* Gainesville, Fla.: Scholars' Facsimilies & Reprints, 1969.

Marx, Leo. *The Machine in the Garden: Technology and the Pastoral Ideal in America.* New York: Oxford University Press, 1964.

Merk, Frederick. *Manifest Destiny and Mission in American History: A Reinterpretation.* New York: Knopf, 1963.

Merritt, Howard. *Studies on Thomas Cole, An American Romanticist.* Baltimore, Md: Baltimore Museum of Art, 1967.

Miller, Lillian B. *Patrons and Patriotism: The Encouragement of the Fine Arts in the United States, 1790-1860.* Chicago: University of Chicago Press, 1966.

Miller, Perry. *The New England Mind: From Colony to Province.* Cambridge: Harvard University Press, 1954.

_____. *Errand into the Wilderness.* Cambridge: Harvard University Press, 1954.

Milner, Clyde A., Ed. *Major Problems in the History of the American West.* Lexington, Mass: D. C. Heath and Co., 1989.

Miner, William H. *Daniel Boone: Contributions Towards a Bibliography of Writings Concerning Daniel Boone.* 1901. New York: Burt Franklin, 1970.

Moore, Arthur Keister. *The Frontier Mind: A Cultural Analysis of the Kentucky Frontiersman.* Lexington, Ky.: University of Kentucky Press, 1957.

Morgan, Charles H., and Margaret C. Toole. "Notes on the Early Hudson River School." *Art in America* 39, no. 4 (December 1951): 161-177.

Mueller-Vollmer, Kurt, Ed. *The Hermeneutics Reader.* New York: Continuum, 1989.

Nash, Roderick. *Wilderness and the American Mind.* 3d ed. New Haven, Conn.: Yale University Press, 1982.

Nietzsche, Friedrich. *The Will to Power.* Translated by Walter Kaufmann and R. J. Hollingdale. New York: Vintage, 1968.

Novak, Barbara. *American Painting of the Nineteenth Century.* New York: Harper and Row, 1979.

_____. *Nature and Culture: American Landscape Painting, 1825-1875.* New York: Oxford University Press, 1980.

Parry, Ellwood C. "Thomas Cole and the Problem of Figure Drawing." *The American Art Journal* 4, no. 1 (Spring 1972): 66-86.

_____. "Thomas Cole's Early Career: 1818-1829." Chap. in *Views and Visions: American Landscape Before 1830.* Washington, D.C.: Corcoran Gallery of Art, 1986.

_____. *The Art of Thomas Cole: Ambition and Imagination.* Newark: University of Delaware Press, 1988.

Pearce, Roy Harvey. "The Significances of the Captivity Narrative." *American Literature* 19, no. 1 (March 1949): 1-20.

_____. *Savagism and Civilization.* Berkeley, Calif.: University of California Press, 1988.

_____. *The Savages of America: A Study of the Indian and the Idea of Civilization.* Baltimore: Johns Hopkins University Press, 1953.

Rash, Nancy. "George Caleb Bingham's 'Lighter Relieving a Steamboat Aground,'" *Smithsonian Studies in American Art* 2 (1988): 17-31.

_____. *The Paintings and Politics of George Caleb Bingham.* New Haven, Conn.: Yale University Press, 1991.

Rathbone, Perry T. *Charles Wimar, 1828-1862: Painter of the Indian Frontier.* St. Louis: City Art Museum of St. Louis, 1946.

_____, Ed. *Mississippi Panorama.* St. Louis: City Art Museum of St. Louis, 1949.

Ravenswaay, Charles Van. "A Rare Midwestern Print." *Antiques* (February 1943): 77-78.

Rogers, Meyric, J. B. Musick, and Arthur Pope. *George Caleb Bingham: The Missouri Artist.* New York: Museum of Modern Art, 1935.

Rusk, Fern. *George Caleb Bingham: The Missouri Artist.* Jefferson City, Mo.: Hugh Stephens, 1917.

Rusk, Ralph Leslie. "The Adventures of Gilbert Imlay." *Indiana University Studies* 10, no. 57 (March 1923): 6-23.

Saxton, Alexander. *The Rise and Fall of the White Republic.* New York: Verso, 1990.

Schaff, Philip. *America: A Sketch of Its Political, Social, and Religious Character.* Edited by Perry Miller. Cambridge: Harvard University Press, 1961.

Shapiro, Michael E., Ed. *George Caleb Bingham.* St. Louis: St. Louis Art Museum, 1990; New York: Harry N. Abrams, 1990.

Slotkin, Richard. *Emergence of a Myth: John Filson's "Boon Narrative" and the Literature of the Indian Wars, 1638-1848.* Ann Arbor, Mich.: University Microfilms, 1966.

_____. "Dreams and Genocide: The American Myth of Regeneration through Violence." *Journal of Popular Culture* 5, no. 1 (Summer 1971): 38-59.

_____. *Regeneration Through Violence: The Mythology of the American Frontier, 1600-1860.* Middletown, Conn.: Wesleyan University Press, 1973.

_____. *The Fatal Environment: The Myth of the Frontier in the Age of Industrialization.* Middletown, Conn.: Wesleyan University Press, 1985.

Smith, De Cost. "Jean François Millet's Drawing of American Indians." *The Century Illustrated Monthly Magazine* 80, new series Vol. 58 (May-October 1910): 79-85.

Smith, Elbert B. *Magnificent Missourian: The Life of Thomas Hart Benton.* Philadelphia: Lippincott, 1958.

Smith, Henry Nash. *Virgin Land: The American West as Symbol and Myth.* New York: Vintage, 1950; reprint, Cambridge, Mass.: Harvard University Press, 1978.

Smith, W. B. *James Sidney Rollins: A Memoir.* New York: De Vinne Press, 1891.

Stehle, Raymond L. "'Westward Ho!': The History of Leutze's Fresco in the Capitol." *Records of the Columbia Historical Society of Washington, D.C., 1960-1962.* Washington, D.C.: Columbia Historical Society, 1963.

Sterven, James E. *Conquering the Frontiers.* La Habra, Calif.: Foundation Press, 1974.

Stewart, Rick, Joseph D. Ketner and Angela Miller. *Carl Wimar: Chronicler of the Missouri Frontier.* Fort Worth, Texas: Amon Carter Museum of Art, 1990.

Stoudt, John Joseph. "Daniel and Squire Boone—A Study in Historical Symbolism." *Pennsylvania History* 3, no. 1 (1936): 27-40.

Sweeney, J. Gray. "Embued with Rare Genius: Frederic Edwin Church's *To the Memory of Cole.*" *Smithsonian Studies in American Art* 2, no. 1 (Winter 1988), 45-71.

_____. "The Nude of Landscape Painting: Emblematic Personification in the Hudson River School." *Smithsonian Studies in American Art* 3, no. 4 (Fall 1989): 42-65.

Taft, Robert. *Artists and Illustrators of the Old West, 1850-1900.* 1953. Princeton, N.J.: Princeton University Press, 1982.

Taylor, Lonn, and Ingrid Maar. *The American Cowboy.* Washington, D.C.: American Folklife Center, Library of Congress, 1983.

Thwaits, Ruben Gold. *Daniel Boone.* New York: P. Appleton & Co., 1902.

Truettner, William H. "The Art of History: American Exploration and Discovery Scenes, 1840-1860." *American Art Journal* 14 (Winter 1982): 4-31.

_____, Ed. *The West as America.* Washington, D.C.: Smithsonian Institution Press, 1991.

Turner, Frederick Jackson. *The Significance of the Frontier in American History.* New York: Holt, Rinehart, and Winston, Rinehart Editions, 1962.

Turner, Justin G. "Westward the Course of Empire Takes Its Way." *Manuscripts* 18, no. 2 (September 1966): 5-16.

Tyler, Ron, Carol Clark, Linda Ayres, and others. *American Frontier Life: Early Western Paintings and Prints.* New York: Abbeville Press, 1987.

Van Noppen, John James, and Ina Woestemeyer Van Noppen . *Daniel Boone, Backwoodsman: The Green Woods Were His Portion.* Boone, N.C.: 1966.

Varner, John Grier, and Jeannette J. Varner. *Dogs of the Conquest.* Norman, Okla.: University of Oklahoma Press, 1983.

Walker, Warren S., Ed. *Leatherstocking and the Critics.* Chicago: Scott, Foresman, 1965.

Wallace, Richard W. *Salvator Rosa in America.* Wellesley, Mass.: Wellesley College Museum, 1979.

Wallach, Alan. "Cole, Byron and the *Course of Empire*," *Art Bulletin* 50 (December 1968): 375-379.

_____. "Thomas Cole and the Aristocracy," *Arts Magazine* 56 (November 1981): 94-106.

_____. "Book Reviews." *Archives of American Art Journal* 28, no. 4 (1988): 21-25.

_____. "Making a Picture of the View from Mount Holyoke." *Bulletin of the Detroit Institute of Arts: The Drawings of Thomas Cole* 66, no. 1 (1990): 35-45.

_____. "Regionalism Redux." *American Quarterly* 3, no. 2 (June 1991): 259-278.

Walton, John. "Ghost Writer to Daniel Boone." *American Heritage* 6, no. 6 (October 1955): 10-13.

Walton, John. *John Filson of Kentucke.* Lexington, Ky.: University of Kentucky Press, 1956.

Westervelt, Robert F. "The Whig Painter of Missouri." *American Art Journal* 2 (1970): 46-53.

White, G. Edward. *The Eastern Establishment and the Western Experience.* New Haven, Conn.: Yale University Press, 1968.

Williams, William Carlos. "The Discovery of Kentucky: Daniel Boone." Chap. in *In the American Grain.* New York: New Directions, 1956.

Wills, Garry. *Cincinnatus: George Washington and the Enlightenment.* New York: Doubleday, 1984.

Wilson, C. K. "Bingham's Bear Cub." *Art Bulletin* 67 (1985): 154.

Wright, Kathleen, Ed. *Festivals of Interpretation.* Albany, N.Y.: State University of New York Press, 1990.

Wright, Nathalia, Ed. *Letters of Horatio Greenough, American Sculptor.* Madison, Wisc.: University of Wisconsin Press, 1972.

Yarnell, James L., and William H. Gerdts. *The National Museum of American Arts Index to American Art Exhibition Catalogues From the Beginning through the 1876 Centennial Year.* Boston: G. K. Hall, 1986.

Checklist of the Exhibition

1. Daniel Boone to Col. William Cristen. Letter 23 August, 1785. The St. Louis Mercantile Library Association.
2. John Filson. "The Adventures of Daniel Boone," from *Kentucke.* (Wilmington, Delaware : James Adams, 1784). Special Collections, Olin Library, Washington University, St. Louis.
3. "Map of Kentucke," from English Ed. of John Filson's *Kentucke.* (Picadilly: John Stockdale, 1793). Special Collections, Olin Library, Washington University, St. Louis.
4. Daniel Bryan. *The Mountain Muse: Comprising Adventures of Daniel Boone, and the Power of Virtuous and Refined Beauty.* (Harrisonburg, Virginia: Davidson & Bourne, 1813). Special Collections, Olin Library, Washington University, St. Louis.
5. Chester Harding. *Portrait of Daniel Boone,* 1820, oil on canvas, 21 1/2" x 16 1/2". Massachusetts Historical Society, Boston.
6. Chester Harding. *Portrait of Daniel Boone,* oil on canvas, 29" x 25". Private Collection.
7. James Otto Lewis after Chester Harding. *Col. Daniel Boon,* 1820, stipple engraving, 13 5/8" x 8 1/8". The St. Louis Art Museum, Museum Purchase.
8. Thomas Cole. *Daniel Boone at His Cabin at Old Osage Lake,* 1826, oil on canvas, 38" x 42 1/2". Mead Art Museum, Amherst College, Mass.
9. Thomas Cole . *Daniel Boone,* c. 1825-6, pencil, pen and wash on paper, 9 1/8" x 8 3/8". Mead Art Museum, Amherst College, Mass., Museum Purchase.
10. James Barton Longacre after Chester Harding. *Daniel Boone,* c. 1838-44, sepia wash on paper, 3 1/4" x 3 5/8". The New-York Historical Society.
11. James Barton Longacre. *Daniel Boone,* line and stipple engraving, 4 5/16" x 3 5/8", from James Herring and James Barton Longacre, *The National Portrait Gallery of Distinguished Americans,* Vol. 2. (Philadelphia: H. Perkins, 1834-1839). The St. Louis Mercantile Library Association.
12. William T. Ranney. *Daniel Boone's First View of Kentucky,* 1849, oil on canvas, 36" x 53 1/2". The Thomas Gilcrease Institute of American History and Art, Tulsa, Okla.
13. William T. Ranney. *Squire Boone's Crossing the Mountains with Stores for His Brother Daniel, Encamped in the Wilds of Kentucky,* 1852, oil on canvas, 31 1/2" x 36". Museum of Fine Arts, Springfield, Mass.
14. Timothy Flint. *The Life and Exploits of Col. Daniel Boone.* (Cincinnati: Morgan, 1850). Special Collections, Olin Library, Washington University, St. Louis.
15 . George C. Bingham. *Pioneer (Flanders Callaway),* 1851 , brush, ink, and wash over pencil on paper, 14 11/16" x 9 5/8". Lent

by the People of Missouri through the Bingham Trust. Acquired through the generosity of Emerson Electric Company.
16. George C. Bingham. *Guide,* 1851, brush, ink, and wash over pencil on paper, 12 1/8" x 9 1/8 " . Lent by the People of Missouri through the Bingham Trust. Acquired through the generosity of Brown Group, Inc. Charitable Trust.
17. George C. Bingham. *Daniel Boone Escorting Settlers Through the Cumberland Gap,* 1851-52, oil on canvas, 36 1/2" x 50 1/4". Washington University Gallery of Art, St. Louis. Gift of Nathaniel Phillips, 1890.
18. Claude Regnier after George C. Bingham. *The Emigration of Daniel Boone,* 1852, lithograph, 18 5/16" x 23 3/4". From the Collections of the Missouri Historical Society, St. Louis.
19. Karl Bodmer and Jean-François Millet. *Capture of the Daughters of D. Boone and Callaway by the Indians,* 1852, lithograph, 17" x 22 2/16". Washington University Gallery of Art, St. Louis. Transfer from Special Collections, Olin Library. Gift in Memory of Mrs. Charles Bryan, Jr.
20. Karl Bodmer and Jean-François Millet. *Deliverance of the Daughters of D. Boone and Callaway,* 1852, lithograph, 17" x 22 15/16". Washington University Gallery of Art, St. Louis. Transfer from Special Collections, Olin Library. Gift in Memory of Mrs. Charles Bryan, Jr.
21. Carl F. Wimar. *The Abduction of Daniel Boone's Daughter by the Indians,* 1853, oil on canvas, 40" x 50". Washington University Gallery of Art, St. Louis. Gift of John T. Davis.
22. Franz Kottenkamp. *Die Ersten Amerikanern in Westen: Daniel Boone und seine Gefahrten.* (Stuttgart: 1856). The St. Louis Mercantile Library Association.
23. Cecil B. Hartley. *Life of Daniel Boone, the Great Western Hunter and Pioneer.* (New York: Lovell, Coryell & Company, 1859). The St. Louis Mercantile Library Association.
24. Emanuel Leutze. *Westward the Course of Empire Takes Its Way,* 1861, oil on canvas, 33 1/4" x 43 3/8". National Museum of American Art, Smithsonian Institution, Washington, D.C. Bequest of Sara Carr Upton.
25. Robert Weir. *"Westward the Star of Empire Takes Its Way" in progress at the Capitol by E. Leutze,* c. 1861, ink on paper, 5" x 7 1/2". Mr. Arthur J. Phelan, Chevy Chase, Md.
26. *Jugend-Album für 1863.* (Stuttgart: Hallberger, 1863). The St. Louis Mercantile Library Association.
27. George Canning Hill. *American Biographies.* (Philadelphia, Pennsylvania: J.B. Lippencott, 1865). Special Collections, Olin Library, Washington University, St. Louis.
28. Anonymous. *Daniel Boone Protects His Family,* 1874, lithograph, 33" x 38". A.G. Edwards, Inc., St. Louis.